ALL OF THE QUESTIONS YOU WANTED BUSH TO ANSWER, BUT THE MEDIA WAS AFRAID TO ASK

ALL OF THE QUESTIONS YOU WANTED BUSH TO ANSWER, BUT THE MEDIA WAS AFRAID TO ASK

✦

BUSH PRESS CONFERENCE QUESTIONS YOU WILL NEVER HEAR FROM THE MOUTHS OF THE REPORTERS OF THE CONSERVATIVE MEDIA

James A. Lukus, Jr.

iUniverse, Inc.
New York Lincoln Shanghai

ALL OF THE QUESTIONS YOU WANTED BUSH TO ANSWER, BUT THE MEDIA WAS AFRAID TO ASK
BUSH PRESS CONFERENCE QUESTIONS YOU WILL NEVER HEAR FROM THE MOUTHS OF THE REPORTERS OF THE CONSERVATIVE MEDIA

iUniverse books may be ordered through booksellers or by contacting:

iUniverse
2021 Pine Lake Road, Suite 100
Lincoln, NE 68512
www.iuniverse.com
1-800-Authors (1-800-288-4677)

ISBN-13: 978-0-595-39040-3 (pbk)

ISBN-13: 978-0-595-83430-3 (ebk)

ISBN-10: 0-595-39040-4 (pbk)

ISBN-10: 0-595-83430-2 (ebk)

Printed in the United States of America

This book is dedicated to George W. Bush because his disastrous policies made this book possible.

This book is designed to answer questions about George W. Bush and his administration by asking questions that should have been asked by the news media during presidential press conferences.

Please read the questions and the articles accompanied with almost every question. By doing this, you will understand how George W. Bush and his administration are using the U.S. government to strip safeguards and rights given to the American people by the U.S. Constitution and Roosevelt's New Deal.

The few questions that are not accompanied by articles are questions that are asked for general insight and therefore are not generated by articles.

Also, this book covers the time frame from the birth of George W. Bush's presidency to November 2005. George and his administration has done much to hurt the United States in the meantime so please be aware that a second or maybe a third volume will be necessary to cover his political exploits after November 2005. I will write those volumes and invite you to send in questions if this book is successful.

Now....read this book and be frightened, disgusted, angry, hurt, and sick and be assured, you will not be bored.

1. President Bush, you said that your life is guided by your Christian beliefs. One of the Ten Commandments says "THOU SHALT NOT KILL", yet as governor of Texas, you broke records in the amount of executions that were performed in your state. President Bush, aren't these executions in direct contradiction to your life of faith?

2. President Bush, your administration put a policy in place that would allow states to limit emergency care of Medicaid recipients. It wasn't until your administration received opposition from Federal law makers that your administration reversed the policy. President Bush, Medicaid recipients are among the poorest and most vulnerable Americans. You have said that your decisions are guided by your faith. Your faith is Christianity. Jesus spent his life helping the poor and the sick. How can your decisions be guided by your faith when your policies are the opposite of what Jesus preached and how he lived his life?

3. President Bush, your administration opposed the use marijuana for medical purposes. It compelled the U.S. Supreme Court to overrule state laws that allowed the use of marijuana by ill Americans. Jesus dedicated his life to healing the sick and easing their pain. President Bush isn't it cruel and against the teaching of Jesus to take away medicine that eases the pain and discomfort of the sick?

4. President Bush, your administration has proposed cutting food stamps by 574 million dollars yet you pushed for billions of dollars to fight the wars in Iraq and Afghanistan. You said that you are a Christian and that your faith guides your decisions. President Bush, would Jesus have approved of your decision to sacrifice starving families in favor of war?

5. President Bush, your administration allows torture in the name of national security. You said that you are a Christian and that your decisions are guided by your religious beliefs. Jesus was tortured in the name of national security because the religious government at the time saw the words of Jesus as a threat to their security. President Bush, Christians believe that the torture of Jesus was not morally acceptable why do you believe that torture is morally acceptable now?

6. President Bush, the bankruptcy reform bill that you signed does not exempt families that are financially devastated by medical bills. You said that your decisions are guided by your faith. One of Jesus' main purposes of life was healing the sick. President Bush, what do you believe Jesus would say about your decision not to exempt families devastated by medical bills from the bankruptcy reform bill?

7. President Bush, you oppose same sex marriage but many Americans can't understand how same sex marriage affects traditional marriages. In their eyes, one has nothing to do with the other. President Bush, do you oppose same sex marriage for religious reasons or do you oppose same sex marriage because your political base wants you to?

8. President Bush, it has been said that your personal Christian faith guides your decisions. One of Jesus' main life purposes was to heal the sick. President Bush, knowing this, isn't your opposition to universal health care a direct contradiction to the teachings of Jesus Christ?

9. President Bush, you have cut funding for Medicaid, Medicare, Section 8, and food stamps among other social programs that help the poor and the sick. These social program cuts hurt the sick and the poor which is just the opposite of what Jesus Christ lived his life for. President Bush, knowing this; why do you believe you get backing from the Christian right? Is the Christian right made up of true Christians?

10. President Bush, you pushed for the adoption of the bankruptcy reform bill. This bill penalizes the poor and middle class for being poor. You said that your decisions are guided by your religious beliefs. Jesus' main purpose in life was helping the poor which is totally opposite of the purpose of the bankruptcy reform bill. President Bush, how can your decisions be guided by your religious faith when your push for the adoption of the bankruptcy reform bill was totally opposite of the purpose of the life of Jesus Christ?

11. President Bush, you said that you are guided by your Christian beliefs and that your decisions are guided by your Christian beliefs yet you are against the use of embryonic stem cell lines outside the ones that you have specified. You know that the use of embryonic stem cells outside the lines you have specified will help

cure diseases. You also know that one of Jesus' main purposes in life was to heal the sick. President Bush, isn't your opposition to the use of embryonic stem cell lines outside the ones you have specified against the teachings of Jesus Christ?

12. President Bush, you cut food stamp funding; funding that helps feed the hungry. You have cut Medicaid funding; funding that helps the sick and the poor. You have cut Section 8 funding; funding that helps shelter the poor. Jesus Christ's purpose in life was to feed the hungry and help the poor. You told Fox News that you pray all the time yet each year you present budgets that cut funding that helps the sick and the poor. President Bush, when you pray, does God tell you to hurt the sick and the poor?

13. President Bush, you supported Republican Senators in their fight to keep Terri Schiavo on life support against her husband's wishes yet you cut funding for the Medicaid program that helped pay to keep her alive on that life support. President Bush, would you have helped Terri Schiavo if her case was not publicized?

14. President Bush, when you were Governor of Texas. You created a law that allowed hospitals and doctors to withhold life-sustaining care from patients that they saw as hopeless. Hospitals and doctors, in Texas, are permitted to withhold patient care even over the objections of the patient's families. If this law was federal, Terri Schiavo could have been taken off of life support by her medical facility or doctor against the objections of her family. President Bush, why have you fought to keep Terri Schiavo alive when, as governor, you passed a law that would have hastened her death? Wasn't your fight to keep Terri Schiavo alive more a matter of political strategy than empathy?

15. President Bush, the price of health care has gone up each year since your administration took office yet your administration has done virtually nothing to keep costs down. In fact, your administration has put through legislation that financially helps pharmaceutical companies increase their profits but does nothing to lower health care costs. President Bush, why isn't lowering the price of health care among your administration's top priorities? How much money has your administration and, or the Republican Party received from pharmaceutical companies during the reign of your administration?

16. President Bush, your administration has blocked legislation that would help ill government weapons workers get compensation for illnesses they incurred while building weapons that are being used to defend the United States. President Bush, why has your administration stood in the way of helping sick American government workers?

17. President Bush, your administration sided with insurance companies to block lawsuits against insurance companies that deny needed services to their customers. President Bush, why has your administration entered into the lawsuits? Has your administration and, or the Republican Party received money from the insurance companies involved in the lawsuits? Has your administration and, or the Republican Party received money from insurance companies in general?

18. President Bush, the states of Missouri, Delaware, Illinois, California, Iowa, and New York have banned the use of thimerosal laced shots and boosters. Thimerosal contains mercury. Studies have revealed that mercury can cause autism in children. President Bush, considering all the research showing the harmful affects of thimerosal and all the countries and states banning the use of thimerosal, why hasn't your administration banned the use of thimerosal throughout the United States?

19. President Bush, your administration pushed for the override of federal law over state law in the case of the use of marijuana for medical purposes. In a recording made by a friend of yours, Doug Wead, you admitted to smoking marijuana. President Bush, since the use of marijuana is part of your past, is it fair that you keep it out of the hands of Americans who need it for medical purposes?

20. President Bush, the cost of health care in America is much higher than it is in countries that have Universal Health Care yet your administration has done little to lower the cost of health care in America. President Bush, knowing this; why are you not in favor of Universal Health Care?

21. President Bush, studies have revealed that mercury can cause autism in children. A vaccine preservative named thimerosal contains mercury and has been suspected of causing autism in the children of parents who sued pharmaceutical companies that used thimerosal. Your administration has moved to block the parent's efforts to receive financial relief for their children. President Bush, why has your administration entered into the legal fight between parents and pharma-

ceutical companies? Has your administration entered the legal fight because pharmaceutical companies are large financial contributors to your administration?

22. President Bush, insurance companies are cherry-picking the Americans they choose to cover. The Americans that remain are the sickest of Americans; Americans that are left out in the cold without medical insurance. President Bush, why doesn't your administration require insurance companies to cover the sick? Why doesn't the government cover Americans that traditional insurance companies won't cover?

23. President Bush, your administration has pushed to soften federal regulations that prohibit the use of human testing of pesticides. These human test subjects include children who cannot make decisions on their own but must rely on adults; and prisoners that can easily be coerced into volunteering for studies by way of threats and offers of freedom. This softening of human testing regulation carries many ethical and moral dilemmas. President Bush, why have you allowed your administration to permit the potential destruction of human lives? Has your administration received political financial contributions from the chemical corporations that make the pesticides?

24. President Bush, your administration has prohibited Medicare from negotiating with pharmaceutical companies for lower prices. This prohibition of negotiation with pharmaceutical companies will cost American taxpayers millions of dollars in lost savings. President Bush, isn't this legislation corporate welfare for the pharmaceutical industry? Has your administration received financial contributions from pharmaceutical companies?

25. President Bush, you are against government sponsored health care like that of Europe and Canada. Considering the rising price of heath care in the United States and the millions of Americans without health care, how will United States citizens be advantaged by not having a national health care program?

26. President Bush, you said that medical law suits should be capped at $250,000 because medical law suits are forcing insurance companies to raise the premiums that they charge doctors, but researchers have found that the main reason insurance companies raise doctor's premiums is because the insurance companies have made bad investments and they are passing those investment losses to doctors by way of insurance premiums. President Bush, are you claiming that high insurance

premiums are being charged to doctors because of large law suit rewards because you actually believe it is the case or because insurance companies are asking you to cap law suit amounts because they want to increase their profits so they can make more investments? Is your administration receiving financial contributions from the insurance industry?

27. President Bush, how does it benefit the American people to forbid Medicare from negotiating with drug companies for lower prices?

28. President Bush, you have said that you want to cap medical law suits at $250,000 because you believe that the amount of law suits are excessive and that insurance companies are raising doctor's premiums because of those law suits but you also said that you want to help Americans pursue a "culture of life". There are many circumstances when $250,000 is not enough to help American citizens pursue a "culture of life". Many times, $250,000 is just the beginning of helping American citizens hurt by malpractice to pursue a "culture of life". They need more than $250,000 to pursue the "culture of life" for the rest of their lives. President Bush, which is more important to you, protecting insurance companies against law suits or helping American citizens pursue a "culture of life"?

29. President Bush, the price of prescription drugs have been going up every year yet your administration will not let Medicare negotiate lower prescription prices like Canada and European Countries do. President Bush, why won't you allow Medicare to negotiate lower prescription prices? Could it be that you don't want to cut into the profits of drug companies?

30. President Bush, you support only specified stem cell lines but you don't support stem cell lines outside those chosen specified stem cell lines. President Bush, if your daughter, or brother, or mother, or father could be helped through research on stem cells outside those that you have approved, would you change your opposition to the use of those stem cell lines?

31. President Bush, while you were in the National Guard, you were never deployed outside the United States because you were in the National Guard and not in the other branches of the armed forces. Do you think it is fair that you sent National Guard members to wars outside the United States when, while you were in the National Guard, no member were sent to a war outside the United States?

32. President Bush, the Senate, led by Republican Senator John McCain put through legislation, 90 to 9, banning the use of torture. Your administration threatened to veto the legislation. This decision to veto Senator McCain's legislation confirms that your administration condones torture. Your administration has spoken out against the use of torture. President Bush, why weren't you truthful about your view of torture? Why shouldn't the international community and the American people conclude that you are a liar when it comes to the truthfulness of your administration's view on torture?

33. President Bush, your administration pushed through the bankruptcy reform bill. Many American citizens are in financial trouble because they lost their job or because of some other financial crisis. These crises cause them to fall behind in their credit card payments. Most of the credit card percentage rates are far above the prime rate. Your administration has done nothing to set a maximum percentage rate that credit card companies are not permitted to exceed. This lack of oversight by your administration will ad to the hardship imposed by your administration's backing of the bankruptcy reform bill. President Bush, why does your administration permit credit card companies to charge sky high rates when you know that the rates will add to the additional financial burden of the bankruptcy reform bill?

34. President Bush, your administration has argued that allowing citizens to sue pharmaceutical manufacturers would undermine public health and interfere with the federal regulation of drugs. In other words, your administration believes that the FDA should not be second guessed. President Bush, knowing this; why should American citizens trust that your administration will fight for their welfare? Why should American citizens trust your administration at all?

35. President Bush, your administration has given Halliburton billions of dollars in no bid contracts to help in the reconstruction of Iraq and your administration gave Halliburton contracts to reconstruct the U.S. Gulf Coast after Hurricane Katrina's aftermath. President Bush, how much has Halliburton paid in U.S. taxes?

36. President Bush, you are in favor of the use of torture. What will you say to countries that torture our captured military personnel when they remind you of your administration's support and use of torture?

37. President Bush, your administration has worked hard to shield pharmaceutical companies from lawsuits. President Bush, without the fear of lawsuits, how will Americans know that pharmaceutical companies maintain rigorous safety measures before they allow their drugs to be released to the public? Why should Americans be forced to suffer for the mistakes of pharmaceutical companies?

38. President Bush, your administration pushed through the Bankruptcy Reform bill that makes it very difficult for Americans to file for bankruptcy. Many Americans who file for bankruptcy do so because of medical bills that they are unable to pay yet your administration has not allowed exemptions for catastrophic medical bills. President Bush, is it morally responsible not to allow exemptions in the Bankruptcy Reform bill for families plagued with huge medical bills?

39. President Bush, the energy bill pushed by your administration does little to decrease the amounts paid by Americans to fill up their gas tanks and to heat their homes, but it does help energy companies who will make billions of dollars in tax breaks and tax incentives. President Bush, was the energy bill pushed through to help the American people or to help increase the profits of energy companies?

40. President Bush, members of your administration has been accused of outing CIA operative Valerie Plame. Many Americans believe that her outing has affected the lives of many CIA operatives who had connections with Valerie Plame and the CIA undercover company Brewster Jennings and Associates. President Bush, has your administration done an assessment of the damage her outing has caused and if so, what were the results of the assessment? How many CIA agents were killed because of her outing?

41. President Bush, your administration suspects Iran of developing weapons of mass destruction. Your administration suspected Iraq of the same thing but your administration chose to use diplomacy with Iran but it chose to use war for Iraq. President Bush, why has your administration chosen to use war against Iraq but diplomacy with Iran?

42. President Bush, some judges and lawyers believe that the constitution does not guarantee the right to privacy. The Patriot Act gives your administration

powers that takes away privacy from American citizens. President Bush, do you believe that the constitution guarantees Americans the right to privacy?

43. President Bush, the Patriot Act allows the CIA to spy on American citizens. This is a power that was never before granted to the CIA. President Bush, why was this power given to the CIA? Wasn't the power to spy on U.S. citizens given to the FBI?

44. President Bush, your administration created the Terrorism Information and Prevention System, known under the acronym, T.I.P.S. T.I.P.S. encourages U.S. citizens to spy on each other. The system is similar to that used by the former East Germany, the former Soviet Union, China, and North Korea. President Bush, how is T.I.P.S. different from that of the oppressive countries of the former East Germany, the former Soviet Union, China and North Korea?

45. President Bush, mothers and fathers of killed soldiers are mourning their son's and daughter's deaths. In response, you said that their sons and daughters died for a noble cause. President Bush, can you explain what that noble cause is?

46. President Bush, your administration has chosen not to participate in the Kyoto agreement. Provisions of the Kyoto agreement may cut into the profits of American energy companies. President Bush, does your administration's choice not to participate in the Kyoto agreement have anything to do with the potential lost profits of American energy companies?

47. President Bush, Hermann Goering, Hitler's right hand man said, "...the people can always be brought to the bidding of their leaders. That is easy. All you have to do is tell them they are being attacked and denounce the pacifist for lack of patriotism and exposing the country to danger. It works the same way in any country." One of your right hand men at the time, Attorney General John Ashcroft said, "to those who scare peace-loving people with phantoms of lost liberty, my message is this: 'your tactics only aid terrorists, for they erode our national unity and diminish our resolve.'". The patriot act, which erodes many civil liberties, was passed after September 11th when American fear was at its peak. President Bush, did your administration use September 11th in the way outlined by Hermann Goering to pass the Patriot Act?

48. President Bush, the Patriot Act allows technology to be used that monitors computer activity down to monitoring email. President Bush, how can you assure the American people that this technology is not being used to monitor the activities of the Democratic Party? Why should the American people believe you?

49. President Bush, you said that one of the goals of your administration is to spread democracy throughout the world. Your family maintains a close relationship with the royal family of Saudi Arabia. Saudi Arabia has been sighted by Amnesty International for human rights violations. President Bush, why has your administration kept close ties with the Saudi Arabian royal family when you know that they participate in human rights violations?

50. President Bush, China is a communist country just as Cuba is yet your administration has an embargo against Cuba but it allows China to hold large U.S. debt and allows U.S. jobs to be outsourced to it. President Bush, why is it acceptable to do business with the communist country of China but have heavy restrictions on business done with Cuba?

51. President Bush, you said that you are against prescription drug re-importation from Canada because you want to keep Americans safe from terrorism but American drug companies make many of their prescription drugs in foreign countries. President Bush, how are you protecting Americans from terrorism by banning drug re-importation from Canada when many prescription drugs are made in foreign countries in the first place? Is the real reason you are against drug re-importation because you don't want to cut into the profits of drug companies?

52. President Bush, on May 22nd, 2003, you made active Presidential Executive Order 13303. The order allows U.S. contractors doing business in Iraq to do business outside the laws of the United States; in essence allowing them to participate in war profiteering with no fear of retribution. President Bush, by signing Presidential Executive Order 13303, aren't you participating in war profiteering?

53. President Bush, most of the attackers of September 11th were from Saudi Arabia. You and your family have had close personal ties to the Saudi Arabian royal family. U.S. citizens who lost family and friends on September 11th attempted to sue Saudi Arabia. Your administration chose to use James Baker to defend the government of Saudi Arabia against the U.S. families. President Bush, why has your administration chosen to defend Saudi Arabia against American families? As

president, haven't you taken an oath to protect the American people against out-side forces? In your eyes, is the welfare of the Saudi Arabian royal family more important than the American people?

54. President Bush, do you believe today's middle class families and lower middle class families can say that they are doing better now than before your administration took office?

55. President Bush, you have pressed for the repeal of the estate tax along with your other tax cuts. The repeal of the estate tax would help the wealthiest 2 per-cent of Americans. The total of these tax cuts will cost the American economy over $5.2 trillion dollars over a ten year period. This $5.2 trillion is money that could be used to strengthen Medicare, help military families, help strengthen the American dollar, and help pay American debts among other things. President Bush, why do you want to cut and repeal taxes that will damage the American economy and hurt the American people? Isn't that irresponsible? Haven't you taken an oath to protect America?

56. President Bush, in 2001, your administration helped Republicans push for massive cuts to flood and hurricane protection programs. In 2003, your adminis-tration cut funds that were needed to maintain flood-control infrastructure in Louisiana. In 2005 Hurricane Katrina devastated New Orleans. President Bush, why did you choose to leave the American people open to the devastation of nat-ural disasters?

57. President Bush, you have pushed for ratification of CAFTA. Many of the countries included in the agreement do not allow the formation of unions and threaten workers with abuse and death. President Bush, why isn't the United State's participation in CAFTA a green light to countries to further abuse their workers?

58. President Bush, you have given the wealthy massive tax cuts at the expense of cutting social programs for the middle class and the poor but members of the middle class and poor make up just about all of the American Armed Forces. President Bush, why should Americans who make up the middle class and poor join the military when your administration is giving away their share of America to the wealthy?

59. President Bush, you had lunch and dinner with Britain's Prince Charles on the day of Rosa Park's funeral. Rosa Parks is an American icon. She gave birth to the civil rights movement. President Bush, why was it more important for you to have lunch and dinner with Prince Charles than attending Rosa Park's funeral?

60. President Bush, your administration repealed a rule that would allow States to use unemployment compensation funds to provide benefits to workers who must leave their jobs to temporarily care for newborn or newly adopted children yet you have come down on the side of right to life groups that are against a woman's right to choose. President Bush, why are you more protective of babies before they are born then after they are born?

61. President Bush, your administration disagreed with the University of Michigan's affirmative action policy that helped create diversity among its students. Along with race and gender, it used talents, geography, athletic talent and other variables to choose which students they would admit yet you were admitted to Yale with grades well below the grades of students Yale usually admitted because your father and your grandfather went to Yale. In other words, you were admitted to Yale via a legacy program. President Bush, wasn't the legacy program that got you into Yale an affirmative action program for the rich? How are legacy programs different from affirmative action programs?

62. President Bush, Nicaragua allows children as young as six to work even though their laws say that children below the age of fourteen are forbidden to work. The Labor Inspectorate of Nicaragua frequently allows the fourteen minimum age law to be broken. President Bush, you pushed for the passage of CAFTA. Why do you want the U.S. to do business with a country that has no clear limit of the minimum age a child must be to work?

63. President Bush, your administration's Council of Economic Advisors has encouraged the outsourcing of American jobs. This outsourcing has caused the loss of millions of American jobs during the reign of your administration. President Bush, why does your administration find putting American workers out of work a good policy?

64. President Bush, your administration opposed expanding Medicaid to the victims of Hurricane Katrina. Many Hurricane Katrina victims were turned away from receiving Medicaid benefits during the height of their suffering. President

Bush, after seeing all the suffering that Hurricane Katrina caused, and remembering the oath that you took to protect the people of the United States, why would you not want to ease the suffering that you saw?

65. President Bush, Nicaragua allows companies to force their workers to work overtime. Workers are forced to work sixteen and twenty four hour overtime days, which translates to forced labor. President Bush, you said that you want to spread democracy throughout the world. You pushed for the ratification of CAFTA. Why would you want to trade with a country that allows what translates to forced labor?

66. President Bush, the Coast Guard is being used as one of the front lines of homeland security yet your administration has allowed its ships and aircraft to fall far below mechanical standards. Mechanical breakdown of these ships and aircraft has gone way up during your administration when they are needed to help keep U.S. ports and waters safe. President Bush, how can homeland security be one of American's top priorities when little effort has been put forth to maintain its effectiveness?

67. President Bush, Porter Goss, head of the CIA said that he knows where Osama Bin Laden is but he won't go after him because he respects the sovereignty of the country Osama Bin Laden is in but your Bush Doctrine says that the U.S. will make no distinction between the terrorists who committed these acts and those who harbor them. President Bush, under your own doctrine, shouldn't you attack the country harboring Osama Bin Laden with no regard to the harboring countries' sovereignty?

68. President Bush, Americans that want to see you when you travel the country are required to sign loyalty oaths. Aren't you the president of **all** Americans? Why should Americans sign oaths to see their President?

69. President Bush, your administration put together a panel to put together a plan to allow private contractors to compete for postal jobs. The United States Post Office is one of the most efficient organizations in the world. They give the most service for the lowest price. This efficiency makes Americans happy. President Bush, why would you want to lower the United States' postal effectiveness by bringing in private contractors? Has the interested contractors donated to your administration and/or the Republican Party?

70. President Bush, your administration pushed for the elimination of ergonomic protections for American workers. This elimination of ergonomic standards was pushed for by the NATIONAL ASSOCIATION OF MANUFACTURERS. Repetitive stress injuries plague hundreds of thousands of American workers each year. President Bush, why would your administration want to push for the elimination of ergonomic standards that help hundreds of thousands of Americans each year? Has your administration and, or the Republican Party received money from the NATIONAL ASSOCIATION OF MANUFACTUERS?

71. President Bush, your administration has used the devastation of Hurricane Katrina to empower the EPA to waive clean air act regulations whenever the agency finds emergency conditions. This will allow corporations to produce poisonous emissions that harm Americans. President Bush, Hurricane Katrina has devastated Americans. Why would you add to the devastation by waiving clean air act regulations?

72. President Bush, you threatened to veto a spending bill if it included an overtime protection guarantee for American workers. Why are you against American workers getting more pay for more work? Did your veto threat have anything to do with the money your administration and the Republican Party receives from industry?

73. President Bush, you want to invest billions of tax payer's dollars to go to Mars yet your administration has saddled American taxpayers with a huge deficit. President Bush, why is the United States going to Mars more important than paying off the national debt and helping the people of the United States?

74. President Bush, your administration helped attack the character of Vietnam veteran and triple amputee Max Cleland even though you nor Vice President Dick Cheney ever risked your lives in defense of the United States. President Bush, how difficult is it for you to sleep at night knowing that you attacked the character of a man who left three of his limbs in a foreign country and who must live everyday with his disability because he risked his life to defend the United States?

75. President Bush, you said that it is better to fight the terrorist over there than over here. The United States' occupying of Iraq has attracted terrorist to Iraq.

President Bush, hasn't your strategy made hundreds of thousands of innocent Iraq citizens targets?

76. President Bush, is your administration free from corruption?

77. President Bush, your 2006 budget proposal grants huge tax cuts to wealthy individuals and Corporations while cutting programs for the poor and middle class. The amount of tax cuts given to wealthy individuals and corporations translate to amounts that are much more than are being paid to keep the wars in Iraq and Afghanistan going. President Bush, why do you believe that the burdens of the Iraq and Afghanistan wars must be carried on the backs of the middle class and the poor?

78. President Bush, the U.S. dollar has fallen in value against the Euro and other currencies. This has caused many investors to abandon the American dollar and invest in the currencies of other countries. President Bush, hasn't the economy that your administration created left the U.S. open to an economic melt down?

79. President Bush, in Panama City, you said that your administration does not torture while, in Washington, your administration via Vice President Dick Cheney fought Republican Senator John McCain's amendment to ban torture and inhumane treatment of prisoners. President Bush, why should the American people and the citizens of the rest of the world believe you?

80. President Bush, Vice President Dick Cheney, acting as a representative of your administration, is pushing for the CIA's right to torture yet while in Panama City, you said that your administration does not torture. President Bush, if your administration doesn't torture, why is Vice President Dick Cheney pushing for torture?

81. President Bush, while in Panama, you said that your administration does not torture but you would not deny the existence of CIA secret prisons that practice torture. President Bush, if your administration doesn't practice torture, why haven't you denied the existence of secret CIA prisons that torture?

82. President Bush, it has been reported that you wanted to privatized Social Security way before you became Governor of Texas and President of the United States. Privatization of Social Security would put money in the hands of stock

brokers which would drastically increase the amount of administrative costs and put money in the hands of people who will profit from their involvement. President Bush, do you want to privatize Social Security to help increase the profits of your financial contributors?

83. President Bush, you said that you don't often read newspapers. How can you understand the people you govern without reading newspapers and keeping up with what's happening outside the beltway?

84. President Bush, you said that you get information about world happenings from objective sources and you said that those objective sources are people from your staff. President Bush, you are the boss of the people of your staff. You can fire them on a whim. How can you be sure that they will give you accurate and objective information if they are afraid of losing their careers?

85. President Bush, how much influence does Karl Rove have on the governing of the United States?

86. President Bush, your administration, via FEMA, awarded Akima Management Services, an Alaskan based company, a no bid contract to supply portable classrooms after Mississippi was hit by Hurricane Katrina. Akima Management Services charged $90,000 per portable classroom. This was double the price of the wholesale price of the classrooms and an amount that was 60% higher than the price Mississippi based companies wanted to charge. Akima Management has connections with your administration and close ties with the former head of the Department of Homeland Security, Tom Ridge. President Bush, did your administration use the tragedy of Hurricane Katrina to steer business to contributors to your administration?

87. President Bush, your administration awarded an Alaskan company a no bid contract to supply portable classrooms to Mississippi after the destruction of Hurricane Katrina. This was in direct opposition to your administration's requirement to give preference to local businesses. President Bush, how can the citizens of the United States and particularly the local citizens of states destroyed by Hurricane Katrina trust that you will keep the promises you make if you find it so easy to break those promises?

88. President Bush, you did not push for the passage of the Central American Free Trade Agreement before you ran for your second term. Did you not push for passage of CAFTA because you knew that it would hurt your chances for re-election?

89. President Bush, in the movie Fahrenheit 911, you were seen making reference to the freedoms of dictators. President Bush, do you envy the powers of dictators?

90. President Bush, Rush Limbaugh has been using prescription drugs illegally yet he has not been sent to jail or even given probation but your administration has come down against the use of marijuana for medical purposes. President Bush, is your administration using its influence to stop the prosecution of Rush Limbaugh because of his backing of your administration on his radio show?

91. President Bush, your administration financially backs abstinence only programs but it does not back programs that include condom use. Experts say that people who practice abstinence only are five times more likely to have oral and anal sex. President Bush, condom use helps prevent sexually transmitted diseases. Why doesn't your administration back condom use for the sake of the health of American citizens?

92. President Bush, your administration has stopped overtime pay for many professions. How does this policy help working families? Did you do this to help increase the profits of employers of the professions?

93. President Bush, Osama Moustafa Hassan Nasr was kidnapped from the streets of Milan Italy by CIA agents on February 17th 2003. Afterwards, he was flown to Egypt where he was reportedly tortured. An Italian judge ordered the extradition of the CIA agents. The CIA agents violated the sovereignty of Italy. The head of the CIA, Porter Gause said that he knows where Osama Bin Laden is but he cannot get Osama Bin Laden because he must respect the sovereignty of the country Osama Bin Laden is in. President Bush, why was it acceptable not to respect the sovereignty of Italy but it is acceptable to respect the sovereignty of the country that is protecting Osma Bin Laden? Isn't the capture of Osma Bin Laden more important than the capture of Osma Moustafa Hassan Nasr?

94. President Bush, in your October 7th, 2002 speech to the people of the United States, you said "we have also discovered through intelligence that Iraq has a growing fleet of manned and unmanned aerial vehicles that could be used to dispense chemical and biological weapons across broad areas. We are concerned Iraq is exploring ways of using UAV's for missions targeting the United States." And you said, "America must not ignore the threat gathering against us. Facing clear evidence of peril, we cannot wait for the final proof—the smoking gun—that could come in the form of a mushroom cloud." At the time, you knew that Saddam Hussein did not have nuclear capability or machines that could fly to the U.S. to deliver these nuclear devices. President Bush, wasn't it your intention at the time to get the country to back your march to war by using fake facts? After this, why should America ever trust you to tell the truth?

95. President Bush, your administration has made deeper budget cuts to the budgets of states that traditionally vote Democrat than to the budgets of states that traditionally vote Republican. President Bush, are you doing this to punish American people who don't agree with your administration's policies and political views?

96. President Bush, under your administration the United States is carrying one of the largest debts in American history. Your administration has cut funding to Social Programs. Your administration has cut funding to the States. Your administration has borrowed huge amounts of money from Japan, China and Saudi Arabia. Your administration has caused more than two thousand American soldiers to be killed and thousands more to be wounded and disabled for the rest of their lives. President Bush, was invading Iraq worth it?

97. President Bush, private employers pay the difference between what reservists made in their private lives and their activated military pay but the federal government acting as employer does not pay the difference. President Bush, why does the government demand that reservist die for this country and become disabled for life for this country but won't help reservists pay the difference in pay that it expects private companies to pay? Why won't the federal government make sure that reservists and their families don't suffer financially because they choose to fight for this country?

98. President Bush, Pat Tillman, former NFL star, was killed in Afghanistan by friendly fire. Your administration via the military said that Pat Tillman died

while leading his troops in battle. President Bush, why did your administration lie to the American people and to Pat Tillman's family? What advantage did your administration seek to gain by lying?

99. President Bush, you agreed to lift your order to suspend the Davis-Bacon Act during the aftermath of Hurricane Katrina. The Davis-Bacon act was put in place to assure that workers receive fair wages and not poverty wages when they are employed by businesses that receive federal contracts. Supporters of your suspension of the Davis-Bacon act say that the suspension was needed to fight inflated building costs but your administration gave no bid contracts to companies that helped build areas devastated by Hurricane Katrina when it knew that money would be saved by forcing companies to participate in the bidding process. President Bush, why is it better to hold down building costs via suspension of the Davis-Bacon Act that assures hard working Americans get fair wages than holding down building costs via the bidding process?

100. President Bush, your administration via the FDA rejected the application to allow over-the-counter sales of the morning after pill. The morning after pill is a great deterrent of teenage and adult pregnancy which would, in turn, avoid huge amounts of unwanted abortions. President Bush, why has your administration chosen to block the sale of the morning after pill when it knows that the pill's use will help avoid abortions?

101. President Bush, you and your administration say that you do not believe that global warming exists yet the other countries that make up the G-8 **do** believe that global warming exists. President Bush, why do you believe that you and your administration in correct and the rest of the G-8 countries are wrong concerning global warming?

102. President Bush, you have done much to stop and slow down the progress of labor unions. Among other tactics, you have negated the safeguards put in place by the Davis-Bacon act that assures workers a fair wage when working for companies that are rewarded government contracts and you have weakened laws that protected unions from companies' efforts to Union bust. President Bush, does this war against unions mean that you don't believe that American citizens should have the right to fight for better working conditions and better pay?

103. President Bush, Bob Jones University has in place many rules that are viewed by most Americans as racist. Few other educational institutions in America use similar rules. You have chosen to visit and give speeches from Bob Jones University on several occasions. President Bush, do you agree with Bob Jones University's perceived racist practices? Have you spoken at Bob Jones University to communicate to your base that you are sensitive to their view on race relations?

104. President Bush, most Americans believe that your administration is heading the Nation in the wrong direction. President Bush, in what direction are you heading the nation?

105. President Bush, you did not push for private accounts to replace current Social Security accounts until after you were re-elected. President Bush, why didn't you push for private accounts during your first term? Were you afraid that your push for private accounts might cost you your re-election?

106. President Bush, your administration via the CDC and the FDA bought vaccines tainted with thimersal, a mercury based vaccine preservative that has been suspected of causing autism in children. The use of thimersal has been phased out by paramedical companies. Your administration sent the thimersal tainted vaccines to third world countries so they can be injected into the bodies of the children in those third world countries. President Bush, why has your administration sent mercury tainted vaccines for use in third world countries when it knows that the injected children may become autistic from the injections? Do you believe that the lives of children of third world countries are less important than that of American children?

107. President Bush, the Supreme Court has ruled against the execution of juveniles who were minors at the time they committed the crime. During your term as Governor of Texas, your State executed more prisoners than any other State in America. President Bush, do you agree with the Supreme Court's decision?

108. President Bush, your administration threatened to veto a spending bill passed by the House of Representatives that pushed to force a $5 billion tax on oil companies but your administration said nothing about vetoing the cuts in social programs that would hurt the sick and the poor. You said in a September 2003 interview on Fox news "Well, I pray daily, and I pray in all kinds of places. I mean, I pray in bed, I pray in the Oval Office." President Bush, when you

prayed, did Jesus tell you to hurt the poor and the sick in favor of making the rich richer?

109. President Bush, a group of pilots who were tortured and abused during the Persian Gulf War in 1991 were awarded nearly 1 billion dollars by a federal judge. Your administration has fought to prevent the pilots from receiving the money but your administration, via Donald Rumsfeld, has said that innocent prisoners that were tortured by your administration in abu ghraib should be entitled to receive financial compensation for the brutal abuse and cruelty they suffered. President Bush, why does your administration believe that American pilots tortured by the hands of the Husein administration is not entitled to financial compensation but prisoners tortured by the hands of your administration **is** entitled to financial compensation? Shouldn't both groups be entitled to financial compensation?

110. President Bush, you chose Kenneth Tomlinson to head PBS. Kenneth Tomlinson has said that PBS is too liberal even though PBS has been praised for its political neutrality. Have you chosen Kenneth Tomlinson to head PBS because you want it to be more sympathetic to your administration's conservative policies? Is assigning Kenneth Tomlinson part of your administration's efforts to make PBS an ally to your administration like Fox News?

111. President Bush, is there ever a reason to take away the civil rights of American citizens for the sake of security?

112. President Bush, your administration allowed 160 Saudis to fly out of the United States immediately after 9/11. Fifteen of the nineteen hijackers who attacked the United States were from Saudi Arabia. Many of the passengers were members of the bin Laden family; relatives of Osama bin Laden. Your administration, via the justice department, did not check the manifests of departing flights against terror watch lists. President Bush, Saudi Arabian citizens and the Osama bin Laden family attacked the United States. Hundreds of Americans were murdered. The people of the United States were traumatized. Why did your administration choose not to keep these potential terrorists in the United States until it was certain that they had nothing to do with the 9/11 attacks? Why didn't you keep your Presidential oath to protect the United States? Why are these Saudis more important than the people of the United States?

113. President Bush, your administration has pushed for cutting the amount of money doctors receive from Medicare. The total amount of money cut from doctor's payments will equal up to 25%. This cut in doctor's payments is at a time when medical costs are rising. Your administration has pushed for cuts that could lead to the elimination of the Medicare. President Bush, has this cut in doctor's payments been made as the next step in the destroying Medicare?

114. President Bush, your administration sends non citizens to countries outside the United States to be tortured yet one of your administration's goals are to spread democracy throughout the world. Your administration does not condone torture by dictators yet your administration participates in torture. President Bush, why is torture acceptable when your administration participates in it but not acceptable when dictators use it?

115. President Bush, on a tape recorded by your friend, Doug Wead, you hinted that you took cocaine as a recreational drug. President Bush, did you ever use cocaine?

116. President Bush, you claim to want to spread democracy throughout the world yet your administration will not follow the rules of the Geneva Convention. Repeatedly, your administration has been caught torturing captured prisoners. President Bush, how can you ask other countries to become democracies when your administration performs torture in direct contradiction of the rules of the Geneva Convention?

117. President Bush, it has been said that your administration made a pact with Saudi Arabia to keep the price of gas low during your re-election run and that the price would go up after your re-election. The price of gas went up more than a dollar just after your re-election. This dollar plus rise, at the time, was the largest jump in gas prices in American history. President Bush, did your administration make a pact with the Saudi Arabian government to hold back price hikes in oil until your re-election?

118. President Bush, you were recorded by a friend of yours, Doug Wead, saying that you smoked marijuana and hinting that you used cocaine. Your White House spokesman, Trent Duffy, revealed that the tape was put in private hands and not given to the White House. President Bush, did your administration

threaten Doug Wead or pay off Doug Wead into putting the tapes into private hands?

119. President Bush, Senators have apologized for past and present Senators for not passing anti-lynching laws. Why haven't you followed their lead and apologized for past presidents who did not push for anti-lynching laws?

120. President Bush, is one of your administration's goals to destroy the Democratic Party and create a one party system?

121. President Bush, Amnesty International has compared the treatment of prisoners in Guantanamo Bay to a Gulag. Members of your administration, including Vice President Dick Cheney, responded negatively to the comparison but none invited Amnesty International to visit the prisoners. President Bush, why haven't you offered Amnesty International open door access to prisoners to prove to the world that prisoner are not being tortured in Guantanmo Bay?

122. President Bush, you joined the National Guard as a young man. Have you encouraged your daughters to join the National Guard and follow in your footsteps?

123. President Bush, while in China, you said that it is not unpatriotic to criticize the Iraq war. You said "People should feel comfortable about expressing their opinions about Iraq." But around the same time, Vice President Dick Cheney said "The suggestion that's been made by some U.S. senators that the president of the United States or any member of this administration purposely misled the American people on prewar intelligence is one of the most dishonest and reprehensible charges ever aired in this city.". When asked if you agreed with Vice President Dick Cheney you said that you agreed with the Vice President. President Bush, were you a hypocrite when you said that it is not unpatriotic to criticize the Iraq war?

124. President Bush, Iran has nuclear facilities that are performing uranium enrichment. The Iran government is not allowing U.N. inspectors to come into the country to assure that the Iran government is not using the uranium to create weapons. President Bush, Iraq was attacked because your administration said that it possessed weapons of mass destruction. Why was it acceptable to invade Iraq because your administration thought that Iraq possessed weapons of mass

destruction but it is not acceptable to invade Iran when it might have weapons of mass destruction? Why was invasion used for Iraq but diplomacy is being used for Iran?

125. President Bush, federal auditors found that your administration paid talk show host Armstrong Williams to distribute propaganda that was favorable to your administration. Has your administration ever given federal funds to the Fox News Network or any of their broadcasters to spread your administration's propaganda?

126. President Bush, anthrax was sent to members of congress. As of yet, the attempted murderer was not found. President Bush, shouldn't this attack on government officials be considered acts of terrorism? Shouldn't your administration continue the investigation until the attempted murderers are caught? Has the investigation been stopped?

127. President Bush, Vice President Dick Cheney told Senator Patrick J. Leahy to fuck himself. Have you confronted the Vice President about his bad behavior? Do you agree with his statement?

128. President Bush, House members have sent you a letter that asks you to respond to issues brought up by the Downing Street Minutes. The Minutes shows that you planned on invading Iraq well before the 9/11 attacks and that you used the intelligence that you received to deceive the American people. President Bush, why haven't you responded to the House letter and challenged the minutes' conclusions?

129. President Bush, do you believe that you are better than middle class and poor Americans?

130. President Bush, in the movie Fahrenheit 911, you said that it would be easier to be a dictator as long as you were the dictator. Your Administration has done much to consolidate power. President Bush, is this power consolidation an effort to mimic the powers of a dictatorship?

131. President Bush, you have pushed for your "no child left behind" program to be used in the nation's public education system and you succeeded yet you have

not fully funded the program. President Bush, why would you push for a program that you are not willing to fund?

132. President Bush, your administration hired the Gilead corporation, the makers of Tamiflu, to supply a vaccine against the bird flu. The former CEO of Gilead was Secretary of Defense Donald Rumsfeld. Donald Rumsfeld made millions of dollars worth of stock from the deal. President Bush, did your administration choose to use Gilead to supply the flu vaccine to Americans because you knew that Donald Rumsfeld would benefit from the deal just as Vice President Dick Cheney benefited from the many no bid government contracts given to Halliburton?

133. President Bush, your administration held Jose Padilla for more than three years in a Navy brig without charging him of a crime. Jose Padilla is an American citizen. He was detained on American soil. President Bush, how is this action different than that taken by dictators of foreign regimes?

134. President Bush, your administration has pushed to shield the Gilead Corporation, the maker of Tamiflu from lawsuits. Secretary of State Donald Rumsfeld was the CEO of the Gilead Corporation. Tamiflu was developed to battle the bird flu and is largely experimental which would make American people who receive the vaccine guinea pigs for the Gilead Corporation. President Bush, what will you say to Americans and their families who might be disabled for life because of the vaccine or what will you say to the family who's family member might die from the vaccine when you tell them that you fought to keep them from getting compensated for their suffering and their losses?

135. President Bush, your administration has tortured prisoners in Guantanamo bay, Iraq, and other locations. Can you think of any circumstance when the torture of American citizens would be necessary?

136. President Bush, you said that your administration would never abuse the powers given to it by the Patriot Act but many of the powers given to your administration by the patriot act allows activities that are not revealed to the suspect or to the public. President Bush, how can you assure the American people that your administration will not or has not abused the powers given to it by the Patriot Act when many of the powers allow for covert activities?

137. President Bush, do you dislike gays and lesbians?

138. President Bush, the budgets that you submitted to Congress cuts funding to states but leaves money in the Federal Government. This trend makes it more difficult for states to maintain state programs. President Bush, are you doing this to consolidate more power within your administration? Isn't this the same tactic used by dictators?

139. President Bush, you said that one of your administration's goals is to spread democracy throughout the world and to use military force if necessary. One of the former Soviet Union's goals was to spread communism throughout the world and to use military force if necessary. President Bush, how is your administration's goals different from that of the Soviet Union's?

140. President Bush, you pushed for the bankruptcy reform bill while you pushed to send jobs out of this country. The American families whose jobs were sent overseas are the same families who were forced to file bankruptcy under the bankruptcy reform laws that you pushed for. President Bush, why did you find it necessary to send American jobs overseas and penalize the Americans that lost the jobs for not being able to pay their bills because of their lost jobs?

141. President Bush, the powers given to your administration by the Patriot Act mirror many of the laws found in dictatorships. How can you tell Americans that you want to stop dictatorships and spread democracy throughout the world when Patriot Act powers written by members of your administration and signed by you support the same injustices practiced by dictatorships?

142. President Bush, what is the maximum amount of soldiers that you believe is too many to die in Iraq?

143. President Bush, you have not written personal letters to all the mothers and fathers of soldiers killed in Iraq. You have not attended the funerals of soldiers killed in Iraq. President Bush, you have found time to push for causes that you believe in and want. Why haven't you written personal letters to the mourning families of dead soldiers that died for one of those causes?

144. President Bush, one of the goals of your administration is to spread democracy throughout the world. Is it morally correct to spread democracy to countries that do not want democracy?

145. President Bush, you said that you want to spread democracy throughout the world yet time after time, your administration has been sighted for human rights violations. When these violations are brought to your attention, you deny them much like dictators and leaders of countries that do not have democracies. President Bush, if you want America to lead in the spread of democracy through out the world, shouldn't America's human rights record be free from any hint of human rights violations?

146. President Bush, you and your family have been blessed with great wealth and power. You have had just about everything you wanted or needed throughout your life. President Bush, your policies have been toxic to the lives of the poor. Have you ever gone out to visit the lives of the poor who are affected by your policies?

147. President Bush, you have pushed to have private accounts replace the current Social Security structure. Wouldn't this help the stock brokers and investment counselors much more than Social Security recipients?

148. President Bush, do you agree with the concept of Social Security?

149. President Bush, you have sent billions of dollars to Iraq; money that could be used here in the United States to build infrastructure, finance social programs for American citizens, help to lower the high cost of health care, and in other ways. President Bush, in your eyes, is Iraq more important than American citizens?

150. President Bush, after being charged with being slow and wrapped up in red tape that contributed to the death of thousands of New Orleans residences, your administration via FEMA, barred the news media from photographing dead bodies recovered in New Orleans after the passing of Hurricane Katrina. President Bush, did your administration stop the photographing of dead bodies because you did not want to add to the negative publicity that your administration had received?

151. President Bush, Donald Rumsfeld ordered the closing of commissaries, the military run stores that offer discounted food and merchandise to low paid military personal and their families. President Bush, why would your administration close stores that help military personal to financially survive?

152. President Bush, your administration gives the most financial help to corporations that donate most to your administration. Your administration gives little if anything to the poor and middle classes that don't donate or are not able to donate to your administration? President Bush, do Americans have to pay to play to get help from your administration?

153. President Bush, Halliburton has been given billions of dollars in contracts by your administration to build in Louisiana after Hurricane Katrina. The main lobbyist for Halliburton is Joseph Allbaugh. Joseph Allbaugh was once your FEMA director and your campaign manager. President Bush, why isn't it a conflict of interest to grant no bid contracts to Halliburton when it's main lobbyist was once a member of your administration?

154. President Bush, the American dollar has dropped against the euro and the currency of other countries during your presidency. This has resulted in the loss of buying power by Americans traveling abroad. President Bush, why should Americans traveling abroad be happy with your administration's handling of the American economy?

155. President Bush, the plunging value of the American dollar against the European Euro has caused American investors and foreign investors to invest in the Euro instead of the American dollar. President Bush, what is your administration doing to reduce this investment trend? Have you or your family invested in euros instead of dollars?

156. President Bush, your administration has done much to restrict and stop the effort of American citizens to get information about your administration under the Freedom of Information Act. President Bush, why does your administration find it necessary to restrict and stop access to information about your administration?

157. President Bush, your administration opted out of entering into the Kyoto agreement. Your decision was said to have been influenced by the Exxon Corpo-

ration, one of the most profitable companies in the world and a company that would benefit from the United States' refusal to enter the agreement. President Bush, why would you allow Exxon, a non-governmental entity, to have so much influence over a governmental decision? Has your administration and/or the Republican party received money from the Exxon Corporation?

158. President Bush, your 2000 presidential campaign focused on personal accountability yet many in your administration has been and is in situations that question their accountability. President Bush, shouldn't you have removed these people from your administration to insure the accountability and honesty of your administration and yourself?

159. President Bush, after Hurricane Katrina passed through New Orleans and victims of Hurricane Katrina were housed in the Astrodome, your mother, Barbara Bush said about the poor who were suffering without homes and were hungry and were mostly African Americans "What I'm hearing, which is sort of scary, is they all want to stay in Texas. Everyone is so overwhelmed by the hospitality. And so many of the people in the arena here, you know, were underprivileged anyway, so this is working well for them". President Bush, do you share your mother's view on the homeless poor who suffered the rampage of Katrina?

160. President Bush, Chief Supreme Court Justice Renquist died during the aftermath of Hurricane Katrina. You chose to set American flags at half mask in respect for his death but you chose not to set flags at half mask in respect for the Americans who were killed by Hurricane Katrina. President Bush, why did you feel that all the American's who died as a result of Katrina were not worthy of setting flags at half mask?

161. President Bush, you have cut Medicaid and Medicare and you have fought against any form of Universal Health care. Almost every G-8 country supplies health care to all of their citizens. In those countries, health care is a right of citizenship. President Bush, why shouldn't every citizen, rich or poor, have the right to have health care supplied to them by the or American federal government?

162. President Bush, female workers who work in Saipan are forced to get abortions by the companies that they work for. Your political base is against abortion as well as your administration's political policy. Also, this practice strips the

women of their civil rights. President Bush, Saipan is an American territory, what is your administration doing to stop this practice?

163. President Bush, women in Saipan are forced to work 14 hour days and live in barracks with one bathroom with tens of other women. As you know, Saipan is a United States territory yet this practice breaks both United States immigration laws and United States labor laws. President Bush, what is your administration doing, if anything, to help these women?

164. President Bush, your administration has come out against the use of medically prescribed marijuana. President Bush, why should sick Americans suffer in their personal lives because of your public political views about marijuana?

165. President Bush, Democrats who have done nothing but identify themselves as Democrats and have been peace loving have been escorted by police out of places at which you or Vice President Dick Cheney appeared. These appearances have been paid for in whole or in part with federal money. The first amendment of the bill of rights says "Congress shall make no law respecting an establishment of religion, or *prohibiting the free exercise thereof; or abridging the freedom of speech*, or of the press, *or the right of the people peaceable to assemble* and to petition the government for a redress of grievances." President Bush, isn't your administration's practice of not allowing Americans to attend your appearances in direct opposition of the first amendment?

166. President Bush, your administration requires citizens who attend your appearances to sign loyalty oaths before they are permitted to attend. Many times, American citizens who do not share your conservative republican ideals are forced from your appearances even though they have done nothing to disrupt and are peaceful. These American citizens need only to identify themselves as Democrats in order to be escorted out. Dictators require citizens of their countries to be loyal and they squash citizens who show decent. President Bush, one of the goals of your administration is to spread democracy throughout the world. Why should countries that don't practice democracy accept democracy when your administration demonstrates practices that are in direct contradiction of democratic ideals?

167. President Bush, Democrats are turned away from events at which you appear. Sometimes they are escorted out of events at which you appear by police

even though they have done nothing to disrupt the events. President Bush, you are president of **all** the American people, including Democrats. As president of the United States, why do you feel that Democrats don't have the right to attend your events and hear your speeches?

168. President Bush, you said that the passage of bankruptcy reform will help the United States. Many American families and individuals seek bankruptcy relief because of some kind of medical catastrophe. American citizens are not clear as to how passage of bankruptcy reform will help them but they do understand how it will help the finance companies that have pushed for bankruptcy reform. President Bush, please explain how bankruptcy reform will help the average American family and individual?

169. President Bush, you have stripped the bargaining rights of federal workers, including those who work in homeland security. You also cut the amount of their yearly pay raise. President Bush, are you working to get rid of federal worker's unions and in turn strip federal worker's rights?

170. President Bush, you pushed for and succeeded in passing a bankruptcy reform bill. The bill does everything to limit the rights of poor and middle class people and families who file for bankruptcy but does nothing to limit the percentage rates that credit card companies are permitted to charge and the amount of the late charges they are permitted to charge. President Bush, why haven't you included percentage rate limitations in the bankruptcy reform bill? How much money has credit card companies donated to your administration and the RNC?

171. President Bush, what place does liberalism have in U.S. government? In your opinion, should liberalism have a place in U.S. Politics and government? Is one of your political goals to rid the United States of liberalism?

172. President Bush, it has been said that Dick Cheney is the brains behind your administration and that you are more of a figure head than a real president that makes decisions. In fact, it has been said that Vice President Dick Cheney runs your administration and makes all if not most government decisions. President Bush, how much and how does Dick Cheney affect your capacity to run your administration and the United States?

173. President Bush, it has been said that Carol Rove, your political advisor is running your administration. It has been said that he is your brain and that you do not make presidential decisions, he does. President Bush, how much does Carl Rove influence your presidential decisions and do you make the decisions?

174. President Bush, what is your definition of conservatism?

175. President Bush, how much more money does your family have now than it did before you became President of the United States?

176. President Bush, during campaigns you have called yourself a "compassionate conservative", but you have cut funding to social programs such as Medicaid, Medicare, Section 8, food stamps, welfare and more but you have pushed through tax cuts that favor the richest Americans and corporations and you have sided with corporations over the welfare of American citizens and you have favored the rich over the middle class and poor in general. Your policies appear to be conservative but not compassionate. President Bush, please define the term "compassionate conservative".

177. President Bush, do you believe that there is any time when it is necessary to lie to the American people and if so, when? Have you ever lied to the American people?

178. President Bush, during your presidential campaign, you called yourself a uniter not a divider but the House of Representatives, the Senate, and the American people are more divided than they have ever been anytime in American history. President Bush, do you still think of yourself as a "uniter not a divider"?

179. President Bush, you reduced the across-the-board basic pay raise of federal employees because you said you wanted to reduce the federal budget but you restored cash bonuses of political appointees of federal agencies. These bonuses were stopped by the Clinton Administration because President Clinton concluded that these bonuses were used to reward political cronies. President Bush, why is it acceptable for you to cut the pay of federal employees that are not federal agency appointees but increase the pay of federal agency appointees by way of bonuses?

180. President Bush, the Senate asked for information to help them make a decision on whether or not to approve John Bolton as Ambassador to the United Nations. Your administration would not give Senate members the information that they requested but your administration did accuse Senate members of blocking Bolton's confirmation. President Bush, why didn't your administration turn over the information that Senate members requested? Shouldn't Senate members get all the information they request so they can make an educated decision on nominations? What did you not want Senate members to know about John Bolton?

181. President Bush, Colin Powell resigned as Secretary Of State and was replaced by Condoleeza Rice. President Bush, was Colin Powell's resignation his idea or was he pressured to leave office by your administration?

182. Colin Powell's son, Michael Powell, resigned from his post as FCC chairman soon after his father, Colin Powell, resigned his position as Secretary Of State of the United States. This is unusual. President Bush, was Michael Powell pressured into turning in his resignation by your administration because of the resignation of his father, Colin Powell?

183. President Bush, Michael Powell was given his position as Chairman of the FCC after his father, Colin Powell, was made Secretary Of State of the United States. Did your administration make an agreement with Colin Powell to make Michael Powell chairman of the FCC if he took the position of Secretary Of State of the United States?

184. President Bush, each year on Memorial Day, you put a wreath on the grave of the Unknown Soldier yet you don't go to the funerals of killed soldiers. President Bush, isn't the ceremony you perform as President of the United States each year on Memorial Day a hypocritical act?

185. President Bush, you headed oil companies before you became Governor of Texas and the President of the United States. You pushed for an energy bill that did nothing to lower gas prices. President Bush, will the passage of this bill help increase your personal wealth after you leave office?

186. President Bush, you broke records in the amount of executions that occurred in Texas while you were Governor. Many of the verdicts were question-

able because of questions involving the defendant's lawyers. In fact, one lawyer slept through much of one of the trials that led to the defendant's execution. President Bush, knowing this, do you regret any of the executions performed in Texas while you were Governor?

187. President Bush, do you believe that your friend and former personal lawyer, Alberto Gonzalez, can put the needs of the American people before you and your administration if he had to make a choice between the two and do you believe that he *should* choose the welfare of the American people before the welfare of you and your administration while he is Attorney General of the United States?

188. President Bush, your mother, Barbara Bush said about the poor who suffered in the aftermath of Hurricane Katrina, "And so many of the people in the arena here, you know, were underprivileged anyway, so this is working very well for them." Did your mother implant this attitude about the poor in you during your childhood?

189. President Bush, Vice President Dick Cheney said about democrats, "American soldiers and Marines are out there every day in dangerous conditions and desert temperatures…and back home a few opportunists are suggesting they were sent into battle for a lie." Vice President Dick Cheney was once the chairman and chief executive officer of Halliburton. Halliburton received several no-bid contracts from your administration to rebuild Iraq and supply services which means that he can profit more from lengthening the war than shortening it. President Bush, Dick Cheney accused democrats of being 'opportunists', why isn't the profits he will receive from the war a product of opportunistic actions?

190. President Bush, the "Downing Street Minutes" shows that your administration had made plans to invade Iraq well before you came to Congress and that you fit intelligence to fit your plans to invade Iraq. President Bush is the "Downing Street Minutes" correct?

191. President Bush, would you be willing to testify under oath that the information and conclusions included in the Downing Street minutes are incorrect?

192. President Bush, Iraq was not infested with terrorists before they were attacked by America but now, after the invasion, Iraq has more terrorist than anytime in history. Terrorists learn their skills in Iraq and use what they've learned in

countries throughout the world. President Bush, hasn't the world gotten more dangerous because of the United States invasion of Iraq?

193. President Bush, your then Secretary of State, Colin Powell, warned you before the invasion of Iraq, that you would have to fix anything that you break. President Bush, considering the billions of American dollars that have been paid to rebuild Iraq, considering the thousands of American lives that were lost in Iraq because of the invasion, considering the thousands of Americans who were injured in Iraq because of the invasion, considering the tens of thousands of innocent Iraqi lives including innocent woman and children that were lost because of the invasion, considering the hundreds of foreign ally soldier's lives that were lost in Iraq because of the invasion and considering the hundreds of foreign ally soldiers that were wounded in Iraq because of the invasion, was the invasion of Iraq worth it?

194. President Bush, in comparison to your administration's efforts in Iraq, little has been done in Afghanistan even though Afghanistan was identified as the origin nation that attacked the United States on 9/11. President Bush, would you have done more in the attack of Afghanistan if Afghanistan contained oil?

195. President Bush, your administration invaded Afghanistan and later Iraq because of 9/11. Your administration created policy because of 9/11 yet you said that you don't think much about Osama Bin Laden, the architect of the attack on the United States on 9/11. President Bush, how can you create policy because of 9/11 without thinking much about the architect of the attack on the United States on 9/11.

196. President Bush, your administration said that the people of Iraq would see the United States as their liberators but instead the people of Iraq see the United States as their occupiers. President Bush, how did your administration get it so wrong in the planning of this war?

197. President Bush, the price of oil has gone up considerably during the Iraq war. How is that possible when the United States possesses control of one of the largest reserves of oil in the world?

198. President Bush, American soldiers have been forced to work with makeshift humvees. The soldiers weld glass, scrap metal, and sandbags to protect themselves

but their efforts are not enough. Many American soldiers fighting in Iraq who are dead and disabled would not be if they had factory installed armor for the humvees. President Bush, why did your administration not send enough factory armored humvees when your administration sent the soldiers to invade Iraq? Did your administration consider factory armored humvees political pork? Did your administration not plan Iraq's invasion as well as it should have?

199. President Bush, most of the 911 terrorists were from Saudi Arabia yet you chose to attack Iraq but not Saudi Arabia. None of the 911 terrorists were from Iraq. You and your family have done business with Saudi Arabia's royal family. President Bush, since many of the 911 terrorist were from Saudi Arabia and none were from Iraq, why did you choose to attack Iraq and not Saudi Arabia?

200. President Bush, was your decision to invade Iraq a mistake?

201. President Bush, your administration bombed Iraq well before it went to Congress to tell them your administration's plans to invade. President Bush, why did you invade Iraq without the backing of Congress?

202. President Bush, when the United States invaded Iraq, your administration said that the invasion would be paid for with Iraqi oil but so far billions of dollars have been invested in the war and no Iraqi oil has been used to offset those billions. President Bush, your administration said that this war would not cost America anything in the way of money. What happened to your promise? Why should the American people ever trust that you will keep your word when you make future promises?

203. President Bush, the "Downing Street Memo" shows that you had planned on invading Iraq long before you came to Congress to seek approval to invade. It also shows that you fitted intelligence to support your plans to invade Iraq. President Bush, do you feel guilty about all the soldiers that were killed and wounded in support of a lie?

204. President Bush, did you plan an exit strategy when you planned Iraq's invasion.

205. President Bush, you have cut funding for VA hospitals while soldiers are coming back wounded from the Iraq and Afghanistan wars. Why would you

slash funding for medical help to soldiers that you sent to protect the United States?

206. President Bush, your administration has cut veteran's benefits in favor of weapon programs but your presidential predecessor, Bill Clinton, did just the opposite. He cut weapon programs in favor of veteran's benefits. President Bush, why do you believe that weapons programs are more important than veteran's benefits?

207. President Bush, your administration increased the amount of money given to Christian groups that have abstinence only programs at the same time you are cutting funds for veterans' health care. President Bush, why do you believe that abstinence only programs are more important than veterans' health care?

208. President Bush, your administration has proposed a $250 annual charge to veterans with non service related illnesses who seek treatment from VA facilities and your administration has proposed closing facilities to veterans with non service related injuries who make more than $26,000 a year, President Bush, why would your administration want to charge our soldiers money for using the VA facilities that they earned the use of and why would your administration cut the use of VA facilities for veterans because they earn a preset amount of money. Haven't these veterans earned the right to use VA facilities where ever and when ever they want?

209. President Bush, your administration was charging soldiers $8 per day for food when they arrived for medical treatment at the Fort Stewart Georgia Base until the practice was protested. President Bush, why would your administration choose to charge injured soldiers for food when your administration knows that the soldiers put their lives on the line for America and were injured while doing so?

210. President Bush, your administration has cut the budget of VA hospitals by billions of dollars. Your administration has made these cuts while knowing that wounded Iraq and Afghanistan soldiers are being added to VA hospital patient lists every week. President Bush, in light of these facts, why has your administration chosen to cut funding for VA hospitals?

211. President Bush, your administration sought to cut imminent danger pay for American soldiers fighting in Iraq and Afghanistan that would add $75 to their monthly paychecks. Your administration also sought to cut $150 a month from active duty soldier's families' paychecks for being separated from their families; money that is badly needed by families here in the United States that are in a financial fight to survive. In fact, these financial supplements were deemed wasteful and unnecessary by your administration. President Bush, why does your administration consider these supplements to active military soldier's paychecks wasteful and unnecessary when these families are trying so hard to make ends meet?

212. President Bush, thousands of veterans are on the streets of America. These veterans have fought for this country and have earned the right to take advantage of all the benefits that America has offered. President Bush, why hasn't your administration made supplying homes for homeless veterans one of your highest priorities?

213. President Bush, you have campaigned that the current Social Security system should be replaced with private accounts. You have said that this reform will benefit young Americans yet you have reduced and cut the benefits of young Americans who enlist in the U.S. armed forces who fight to defend the freedoms of the United States. President Bush, why should young Americans trust that you have their best interest in mind in regard to their future when you don't have their best interest in mind in regard to them risking their lives to defend America?

214. President Bush, your administration hired the Lincoln Group, a Washington based public relations firm, to write articles in Iraq newspapers without the knowledge of the Iraqi people. The articles are a form of propaganda that is practiced only in countries that do not practice democratic principles. President Bush, why have you, who have preached for the spreading of democracy throughout the world, turned your back on one of the bedrocks of true democracy?

215. President Bush, your administration created a policy that does not allow coffins coming back from the wars in Iraq and Afghanistan to be photographed. Your administration said that this policy was put in place to help the families of killed soldiers. President Bush shouldn't the families of killed soldiers and not government have the right to decide whether or not they want their loved one's coffins to be photographed?

216. President Bush, military recruiters target schools in poor neighborhoods much more often than they target schools in more affluent neighborhoods. Why? Are children of poorer families more expendable than children of affluent families?

217. President Bush, Halliburton charges many times more per gallon for fuel than the British company Lloyd-Owen. Both companies are contractors in Iraq and follow similar routes. President Bush, why should the American taxpayer pay many times per gallon more for fuel than the amount paid by British taxpayers? Shouldn't Halliburton be forced to charge fuel amounts comparable to Lloyd-Owen?

218. President Bush, almost every great empire or nation that tried to fight extensive wars that drained their economy eventually collapsed. The United States is paying billions of dollars per month to fight the wars in Iraq and Afghanistan with no end in sight. President Bush, aren't you concerned that the United States will share the same fate as the great empires and nations before it?

219. President Bush, KBR a subsidiary of Halliburton which was once run by Vice President Dick Cheney, claimed to have fed more soldiers than it actually fed. President Bush, why haven't you fired KBR for this and had the justice department prosecute its management?

220. President Bush, KBR a subsidiary of Halliburton, hired a Kuwaiti subcontractor to supply meals to American soldiers. President Bush, why hasn't your administration saved American taxpayers money by hiring the Kuwaiti company directly?

221. President Bush, you said, "The United States is committed to the worldwide elimination of torture and we are leading this fight by example. I call on all governments to join with the United States and the community of law abiding nations in prohibiting, investigating, and prosecuting all acts of torture and in undertaking to prevent other cruel and unusual punishment." You said this while the U.S. was torturing people in Iraq and other world locations. President Bush, you knew that this commitment to torture elimination by the United States was untrue. Aren't you giving other countries the O.K. to torture but deny they are

torturing? Shouldn't countries prohibit, investigate and prosecute all acts of torture by your administration?

222. President Bush, KBR a subsidiary of Halliburton, served American soldiers in Iraq food that was more than a year old. This was done with the full knowledge of KBR management. President Bush, why hasn't your administration fired KBR and replaced it with a company that will do what American tax payers pay them to do?

223. President Bush, you gave covert directives to set up secret interrogation facilities for the purpose of using new harsher methods of interrogation which most if not all countries of the world would consider torture. You sent out those directives at the same time you were telling the rest of the world that you denounced torture. President Bush, weren't you being a hypocrite when you denounced torture at the same time you were promoting torture?

224. President Bush, many terrorists come into Iraq by way of its borders. One of the countries bordering Iraq is Saudi Arabia, the same country most of the 9/11 terrorist were from and a U.S. ally. President Bush, if Saudi Arabia is such a good ally of the United States, why does it allow terrorists to cross its border into the Iraq? Why hasn't your administration made an agreement with Saudi Arabia to increase the guarding of the Saudi Arabian Iraq border?

225. President Bush, your administration has not provided troops in Iraq and Afghanistan with Kevlar Body Armor. Instead your administration has left it up to the families of the soldiers to provide the armor. President Bush, with all the money invested in the reconstruction of Iraq, why would your administration not find the lives of the soldiers fighting in Iraq and Afghanistan worthy of the protection provided by Kevlar Body Armor?

226. President Bush, Saddam Hussein has tortured the people of Iraq and your administration has allowed the torture of the people of Iraq. President Bush, as far a torture is concerned, how are you better than Saddam Hussein?

227. President Bush, your administration did not supply enough armored humvees to Iraq. As a result, thousands of service men and women have been killed or wounded. If your administration had supplied factory installed armored humvees, many of the deaths and wounds of American soldiers would have been

avoided yet defenders of your administration's decisions has said that armor slows down the humvees and is a strain on their transmissions. They also say that the armor does not fully protect the humvees occupants. President Bush, do you accept these excuses as valid and do you believe that these reasons are sound enough to curtail the production of factory installed armor for military humvees?

228. President Bush, there are shortages of factory installed medium and heavy weight armored trucks as well as a shortage of factory installed armored humvees but the shortages of medium and heavy factory installed armored trucks far outweigh that of factory installed armored humvees . These medium and heavy weight trucks are used to transport food, fuel and supplies that are vital to the American troops in Iraq. President Bush, your administration has done everything but ignore the need for armored medium and heavy trucks and their openness to attack by roadside bombs, why hasn't your administration done more to armor these trucks and protect the lives of American troops?

229. President Bush, Donald Rumsfeld, your defense secretary, said that he expects the United States to be at war in Iraq for as much as twelve years. That would mean that today's seven and eight year olds could be fighting, dieing, and disabled for life before they have a chance to see what life is. President Bush, isn't this Iraq war turning into another Vietnam?

230. President Bush, your administration took advantage of stop loss measures that force members who are out of the Reserve back into active duty. These service men and women were honorably discharged and have started families and careers and many have retired. President Bush, is your administration going to continue using stop loss to pull honorably discharged men and women from their families, careers, and retirement to fight the war in Iraq? Do you believe this is fair to the men and women who already risked their lives and put their lives on hold to defend and fight for this country?

231. President Bush, your administration's use of stop loss endangers the lives of military personnel past the years included in their contracts. This means that a soldier who signed a contract to stay in the military for two years but has to stay in the military for three years under stop loss has an excellent chance of dying or getting injured during the additional year that stop loss forces them to serve. President Bush, do you believe that this is fair to the troops that serve our country and if so, why?

232. President Bush, how many U.S. Troops were killed or injured after being forced to stay on active duty because of your administration's use of stop loss?

233. President Bush, enlistment and re-enlistment quotas have not been met for months and years. Your administration has persistently used stop loss to maintain troop numbers in Iraq. President Bush, does your administration's extensive use of stop loss have anything to do with the low enlistment and re-enlistment numbers suffered by the military?

234, President Bush, Iraq contractors have been found to have engaged in war profiteering such as charging the American taxpayer for meals that were not served, for serving food that was spoiled, for over charging for rendered services and products and in other ways. President Bush, doesn't this equate to making profit off of the lives of our troops? What is your administration doing to stop war profiteering? Since Vice President Dick Cheney was the CEO of one of the major war contractors and still might have ties to that war contractor, did he have anything to do with allowing war profiteering to occur?

235. President Bush, your administration has been suffering from its inability to meet recruitment quotas. Your administration has been using stop loss extensively to maintain troop numbers in Iraq. President Bush, does your administration's inability to meet recruitment quotas and lack of ability to maintain troop numbers have anything to do with your administration's poor military planning?

236. President Bush, Iraq private contractors such as Halliburton and KBR and Blackwater are not part of the military chain of command. They can refuse to perform services if they believe that situations are too dangerous or for any other reasons. This can force military personnel to perform vital duties without the backing of hired contractors leaving military personnel open to be killed or badly injured. President Bush, why isn't vital services being performed within the military chain of command to assure the safety of our troops?

237. President Bush, the average pay for an enlisted E2 Army soldier is just under $16,000 a year as opposed to civilian contractor employees that can make over $100,000 a year. President Bush, doesn't this huge pay inequality cause undo frustration and demoralization to the average enlisted military member who, at times, has to work side by side with private contractor employees?

238. President Bush, why should the American people trust that your administration will not abuse the powers given to it by the Patriot Act?

239. President Bush, your administration has been using cell phones to track Americans and as a tool for surveillance. You are pushing to do this without court orders and without probable cause which raises Fourth Amendment concerns. President Bush, why should the American people give up their Fourth Amendment rights for the sake of your administration's wish for unrestrained powers?

240. President Bush, your administration has made an agreement with Wal-Mart. The agreement gives Wal-Mart a 15 day notice before labor inspectors inspect stores for child labor violations. Of course this 15 day notice gives Wal-Mart plenty of time to clean up its act before inspection. President Bush, why would your administration make such an agreement? Are you in favor of child labor?

241. President Bush, you allowed Michael Brown to stay to continue receiving his reported $148,000 annual salary 30 days after your administration encouraged him to step down has head of FEMA; in essence rewarding him for his incompetence. President Bush, why shouldn't the victims of Hurricane Katrina be angered at this?

242. President Bush, Michael Brown had no formal emergency management experience. Why did you appoint him as FEMA Director?

243. President Bush, Michael Brown, former head of FEMA has started an emergency planning consulting business. Michael Brown stepped down as head of FEMA because of the ineptitude he showed in responding to the Hurricane Katrina disaster. President Bush, do you believe it is fair that Michael Brown financially benefit from the horrible mistakes he made in responding to the Hurricane Katrina disaster?

244. President Bush, you said in a November 2005 radio address, "This week we also extend our gratitude to our military families, who are making great sacrifices to advance freedom's cause. They can know that we will honor that sacrifice by completing the noble mission for which their loved ones gave their lives." President Bush, since these families will never see their loved ones again and since they

will know that their loved ones died a horrible death, why haven't you found the time to send each family a hand written letter thanking them for their family's sacrifice?

245. President Bush, in a November 2005 radio address you said, "Many of our servicemen and women have endured long deployments and separations from home....Those they leave behind must deal with the burden of raising families while praying for the safe return of their loved ones." President Bush, what has your administration done to make the sacrifice of these families easier?

246. President Bush, Vice President Dick Cheney was CEO of Halliburton. Halliburton is one of the main contractors your administration hired to help with services in Iraq. Halliburton is also the parent company of KBR, another company hired by your administration to help with services in Iraq. Halliburton and KBR were hired without being forced to bid on the projects. This means that the United States government may not have received the lowest price for services. President Bush, did Dick Cheney's ties to Halliburton and its subsidiaries have anything to do with your administration's choice to not require Halliburton to bid on the contracts?

247. President Bush, your administration has been accused of trying to prevent Americans from seeing daily images of death that could sour support for the Iraq war. This criticism was sparked by your administration's policy of not permitting flag draped coffins from being photographed. President Bush, are these criticisms true?

248. President Bush, thousands of American soldiers have been killed in Iraq and for each soldier that is killed, tens of people are affected in the United States more or less including the soldiers' children and wives and mothers and fathers. President Bush, what is the maximum number of soldiers and families you are willing to sacrifice for the purpose of completing your administration's plans for Iraq?

249. President Bush, Halliburton, KBR, Blackwater and other contractors were forced to do little or no bidding to get Iraq contracts yet they were hired to lower the cost to American taxpayers. President Bush, since these companies had to do little or no bidding, what reason do they have to keep the prices they charge American taxpayers low?

250. President Bush, you said that the soldiers in Iraq are giving their lives for a noble cause. Have you spoke with your daughters about risking their lives for that noble cause. If not, why not?

251. President Bush, you said that the soldiers in Iraq are giving their lives for a noble cause. Have you encouraged Congressmen and Congresswomen and members of your administration to encourage their sons and daughters to risk their lives for that noble cause? If not, why not?

252. President Bush, many Iraqis are being tortured in Guantanamo Bay and American facilities in Iraq. This is a direct violation of the rules of the Geneva Convention. President Bush, how can the United States expect captured American soldiers to be protected by the rules of the Geneva Convention when the United States itself does not follow the rules of the Geneva Convention and do you care that captured American soldiers may not be protected by the rules of the Geneva Convention because of your administration's torture policies?

253. President Bush, your administration has done much to further the investigation of the "oil for food" scandal at the United Nations but your administration will not investigate the loss of over eight billion dollars in Iraq. President Bush, why has your administration determined that the "oil for food scandal" is more important than the over eight billion dollars that has been lost in Iraq? Why won't your administration fight to find out what happened to the eight billion dollars lost in Iraq and jail the wrong doers?

254. President Bush, your administration via the Justice Department conducted an investigation of the outing of the National Security Agency's surveillance of U.S. citizens without court orders. This has led to questions about your over reach of presidential powers and the legality of your actions. President Bush, the news media has an obligation to investigate the government. By launching this investigation, are you attempting to intimidate the news media from fulfilling that obligation?

255. President Bush, former Attorney General John Ashcroft refused to approve key parts of your program to allow the federal government to spy on American citizens. In fact, your then Chief of Staff Andrew Card and now Attorney General Alberto Gonzales visited John Ashcroft at his hospital bed in an effort to persuade him to approve the parts of the project that he refused to sign off on. Not

long after that, he resigned as Attorney General of the United States. President Bush, did John Ashcroft's decision to not fully back your spy program have anything to do with his decision to leave your administration? Did you push for John Ashcroft's resignation?

256. President Bush, there has been many instances when Iraq military contractors have been caught overcharging American taxpayers and charging American taxpayers for services that were not performed. This translates to war profiteering. President Bush, what is your administration doing to stop war profiteering?

257. President Bush, you pushed for the bankruptcy reform bill that makes it more difficult for Americans to file for bankruptcy. President Bush, won't the passage of this bill discourage Americans from starting small businesses?

258. President Bush, you pushed through and signed the Bankruptcy Reform Act that makes the requirements of bankruptcy more severe for Americans who file bankruptcy. The reported reason why you and congress pushed for this act is to make Americans more financially responsible yet your financial policies has plunged America into a huge deficit. President Bush, isn't your push for bankruptcy reform and making Americans more financially responsible hypocritical? Hasn't your administration's fiscal policies proven that you are irresponsible?

259. President Bush, in 2004, your administration supported the Michigan Secretary of State's argument that provisional ballots can be rejected if voters voted at the wrong polling place. This was after redistricting which caused many voters to not know the location of their polling place. President Bush, why would you want to keep Americans from voting? Shouldn't all eligible Americans have the right to vote? Was this your administration's tactic to restrict the votes of voters that were not voting Republican?

260. President Bush, you were given a surplus when you took office. You turned the surplus into a deficit. President Bush, knowing this; why should the American people trust that you know best when dealing with Social Security?

261. President Bush, you pushed for your no child left behind program but you refuse to fund it properly. President Bush, is this your way of destroying public education in America?

262. President Bush, you pushed for passage of the bankruptcy reform bill that makes it much more difficult for middle class and poor Americans to file for bankruptcy but the bill does nothing to limit the percentage rate that lenders are permitted to charge. President Bush, why are you allowing lending companies to charge loan shark percentage rates?

263. President Bush, you have made several cuts to community oriented policing services that provide state and local grants to hire police officers in American cities yet you said you want to protect America from terrorism. President Bush, how can you protect America from terrorism if you do not have enough police on the front line to protect America from terrorism?

264. President Bush, you insisted that homeland security employees have no collective bargaining rights or civil service rights. You said that these stripping of rights were necessary because you wanted to create management flexibility. President Bush, considering your past opposition to unions, was your opposition to homeland security employee rights born more out of your dislike of unions more than your wish to improve homeland security?

265. President Bush, under your administration, the United States is financing a huge deficit. Aren't you afraid of bankrupting the country and creating a depression?

266. President Bush, six traffic controllers provided accounts of their communications with hijacked planes on September 11th. The tape was not copied. It was destroyed by a Federal Aviation Administration Manager. The FAA said that the destruction of the tape was done in error but an FAA manager said that he destroyed the tape by crushing it with his hand, cutting it into small pieces and depositing the pieces into trash cans around the building. President Bush, the description of the destruction of the tape does not sound like it was an accident. Was FAA managers given orders from your administration to destroy those tapes?

267. President Bush, months after the devastation of Hurricane Katrina, poor Americans were still being moved from place to place while fighting everyday to survive yet you are sending billions of dollars to Iraq. President Bush, why is the welfare of the citizens of Iraq more important than the citizens of the United States?

268. President Bush, your administration has invested millions of dollars of federal money in abstinence only programs even though studies have shown that programs that do not include condom use are ineffective when it comes to slowing down teen pregnancy. President Bush, why is your administration investing federal money into abstinence only programs that are ineffective?

269. President Bush, the Constitution considers the three branches of government as co-equals. Do you agree with this or do you believe that the President of the United States should be more powerful than the other two branches of government?

270. President Bush, corporations avoid paying federal taxes by using accounting maneuvers. This translates to trillions of dollars every year that are not collected by the federal government. The United States is carrying the largest deficit in history. President Bush, why hasn't your administration closed the accounting loop holes that allow corporations to avoid paying taxes?

271. President Bush, during your governorship of Texas from 1995 to 2000, Texas was one of the top five states with the most teen pregnancies. This was at the same time that Texas had abstinence only programs that did not include the use of condoms to prevent pregnancies. Studies have shown that abstinence only programs are ineffective without teaching the proper use of condoms. As president, you spread abstinence only programs throughout the fifty states. President Bush, why would you put federal money into programs that were ineffective in Texas and spread them throughout the U.S. where they are continuing to be ineffective?

272. President Bush, the District Of Columbia does not have a voting Representative in the United States House of Representatives which means that the United States citizens who live in the District Of Columbia does not have a voice in what the Federal Government does yet on many occasions, the United States House Of Representatives gets involved in local D.C. politics. President Bush, don't you agree that all U.S. citizens should have a voice in the federal government?

273. President Bush, there are many conservatives that believe that gays and lesbians should not be permitted to adopt children. Do you agree with them?

274. President Bush, most African American voters feel that they were kept away from the voting polls in Ohio. Among other voting complaints, many African American voters had to stand in long lines to vote while white voters lines were short. As you know, African Americans vote overwhelmingly for Democrats. President Bush, did your administration and the Republican Party disrupt the African American vote in Ohio?

275. President Bush, the American people know that you are against gay and lesbian marriage. Should gays and lesbians have the right to enter into civil unions?

276. President Bush, the citizens of the District of Columbia do not have a Representative in the United States House Of Representatives. This means the District of Columbia has no voice in the federal government. African Americans make up a large portion of the population of the District of Columbia. The bulk of African Americans vote Democrat. You have done nothing to give DC residents a voice in the federal government. President Bush, would you fight more to give DC residences a voice in the federal government if they traditionally voted Republican?

277. President Bush, should the issue of homosexuality be banned from discussion in high school sex education classes?

278. President Bush, your administration has cut funding to local governments for law enforcement. You have fought to strengthen the powers of the Patriot Act because you said that it will help protect the American people against terrorism. You know that local law enforcement is the first line against terrorism. President Bush, why has your administration cut local funding for local law enforcement when you know that local law enforcement is the first line against terrorism?

279. President Bush, corporations that are awarded federal contracts are permitted to avoid paying federal taxes. President Bush, why should corporations receive federal tax money via federal contracts if they don't pay their share federal taxes?

280. President Bush, in October 2004 you signed a tax-cut bill that gave large cuts to corporations by way of tax cuts and deductions. The majority of these tax cuts and deductions were given to corporations that have ties to lawmakers. President Bush, why have you done this when you know that the United States is suf-

fering through a huge deficit? Why have you put the welfare of corporations before the welfare of the American people?

281. President Bush, your administration has cut funding to the Small Business Administration. The Small Business Administration backs the micro loans that help in the creation of blossoming small businesses. President Bush, on many occasions, you have spoke of the importance of small businesses in the American economy. Why would you cut funding to help create small businesses when you know that small businesses help the American economy?

282. President Bush, in the economy that your administration has created, Americans must work 2 or 3 jobs to make ends meet. What have you done to alleviate this situation?

283. President Bush, in Georgia, parents of high school students barred the forming of a high school club made up of gay and straight students. Since Georgia is a red state, most of the parents probably voted for you. President Bush, do you think this promotes hatred between the gay and straight worlds? Shouldn't this High School club be seen as an opportunity to help build acceptance in the hearts of young people?

284. President Bush, the lovers of gays and lesbians want to be permitted to act as legal representatives for their sick lovers. Many members of your Christian base don't believe that gays and lesbians should have that right. President Bush, do you agree with your Christian base? Do you believe that gays and lesbians should not have the right to act as legal representatives for sick lovers?

285. President Bush, many of your policies will cost the young of today billions and even trillions of dollars when they are old enough to pay taxes and raise their families. President Bush, do you consider this fact when you create policies?

286. President Bush, you pushed for and passed the Patriot Act after the 9/11 attack on the United States when American citizens' fears were at their highest. President Bush, would you have attempted to pass the Patriot Act if the 9/11 attack never happened? Were you exploiting the fears of the American people to get the Patriot Act passed?

287. President Bush, many people believe that the poor and middle classes are here in America to serve the rich and your administration's efforts to cut taxes for the rich while cutting social programs and encouraging American jobs to be sent overseas supports this view. President Bush, do you believe that the poor and middle classes are here in America to serve the rich?

288. President Bush, your Attorney General, Alberto Gonzalez was your personal lawyer. Knowing this; how can the American people be assured that, as Attorney General of the United States, he will put the needs of America before your personal needs? How can the American people be assured that he can perform an honest investigation of you and your administration if the occasion arises?

289. President Bush, your tax cuts benefit the wealthy and super wealthy but they do very little for the middle and poor classes. The rich has the financial means to buy just about anything they want when they want it but the middle class and poor must monitor their budget closely to make sure they don't over spend. Also there are more middle class and poor people than wealthy and super wealthy people. This means that middle class people and the poor can do more to strengthen the economy than the wealthy and the super wealthy. President Bush, knowing this; why is it more important to put money in the hands of the wealthy and the super wealthy than in the hands of the middle class and the poor?

290. President Bush, your mastery of the English language is much more limited than American Presidents before you. Is this lack of ability a hindrance to your ability to do your job as President of the United States?

291. President Bush, the CEO of the Diebold Corporation which made many of the voting machines that were used during your 2004 re-election, vowed that he would support and help you pursue your re-election bid. President Bush, wasn't that a conflict of interest and a blow to the pursuance of a fair and transparent election? Shouldn't the United States bar the use of Diebold voting machines on all government levels and if not, why not?

292. President Bush, after Hurricane Katrina devastated areas of Alabama, Florida, Louisiana and Mississippi, you issued an executive order that suspended the Davis-Bacon Act. The Davis-Bacon Act set a minimum pay scale for workers employed by companies that were granted government contracts. You did nothing to cap the profits of oil companies and the contractors that made record prof-

its from the devastation. President Bush, why was it important for you to limit the amount of wages workers received for rebuilding their communities but it was not important to limit the profits of companies born from the misery of Hurricane Katrina's devastation?

293. President Bush, hundreds of thousands of Americans don't have health care insurance and many of those who don't have health care insurance die because they are not able to afford health care. Most of the G-8 countries have national health care for their citizens. President Bush, what advantage does the United States have over countries that have national health care by not having national health care? Why is it important that the United States not have national health care?

294. President Bush, your administration received much harsh criticism about FEMA's inadequacies in responding to the aftermath of Hurricane Katrina. Much if not most of U.S. citizens believed that more lives would have been saved if FEMA would have responded in a more responsive manner. The director of FEMA, Michael Brown was relieved of his duties but he was not fired. President Bush, why would your administration choose not to fire Michael Brown? By not firing Michael Brown, weren't you telling the American people that political ties and personal ties are more important than the welfare of the American people you have sworn to protect?

295. President Bush, after the tragedy of Hurricane Katrina, you called for Congress to OK over 60 billion dollars in aid. Congress passed the Hurricane Katrina aid package. The combination of the Hurricane Katrina package along with the amount being paid to maintain the war in Iraq has caused great strains on the U.S. economy. President Bush, considering the burden these billions of dollars has on the average American tax payer and the strain it has on the U.S. economy, will you consider rolling back the tax cuts you put in place to help the top 20 percent of American taxpayers?

296. President Bush, you pushed for passage of the bankruptcy reform bill. The bill was pushed by finance corporations and makes it more difficult for American citizens to file for bankruptcy yet it does nothing to stop finance corporations from charging American citizens loan shark like interest rates. President Bush, why should the American people who suffered because of your bankruptcy bill back you and the Republicans who voted for the bill?

297. President Bush, items made in Saipan are permitted to say that they are made in America even though the items are not being made in any of the 50 states. President Bush, isn't this a deceptive practice? Shouldn't items made in Saipan say that they are made in Saipan?

298. President Bush, your No Child Left Behind program has caused schools to be forced to lay off teachers, has caused over crowding in classes, has caused schools not to be able to afford text books, and has caused other difficult education situations. President Bush, knowing this; why haven't you re-evaluated the effectiveness of the program? Why haven't' you done more to adequately fund the program?

299. President Bush, your No Child Left Behind program can cause school districts to be taken over by private companies. Was the rules of the No Child Left Behind program put in place to force the federal and state governments to replace our current public school structure with a privately owned school structure?

300. President Bush, when hurricane Katrina hit New Orleans you were on vacation. You stayed on vacation during the aftermath of Katrina and flew back well after rescue efforts should have been started. President Bush, why didn't you cut your vacation short and fly back to the white house before Katrina hit?

301. President Bush, Vice President Cheney arrived in New Orleans and the rest of the area devastated by Hurricane Katrina ten days after it hit. This was one of the largest disasters in American history. President Bush, why did Vice President Cheney choose to stay on his vacation and wait two weeks to respond to the disaster? Why didn't you insist that he cut his vacation short for the good of the people of the United States?

302. President Bush, you appointed Michael Brown to head FEMA. Before his appointment, he was commissioner of the International Arabian Horse Association. President Bush, how did heading the International Arabian Horse Association prepare Michael Brown to head FEMA?

303. President Bush, most of the American people believed that your administration responded terribly to the aftermath of Hurricane Katrina. Your administration's response to Hurricane Katrina has caused many Americans to question

your administration's ability to respond to terrorist attacks. President Bush, why should the American people be confident in your administration's ability to respond to terrorist attacks when they have seen your administration's inability to respond well to the aftermath of Hurricane Katrina?

304. President Bush, under No Child Left Behind, children from richer neighborhoods get better educations than children from poorer neighborhoods because parents of children from richer neighborhoods are better able to fund their children's education. This leaves children from poorer neighborhoods at a vast learning disadvantage. President Bush, why hasn't your administration done more to close this learning gap? Do you want to close the learning gap?

305. President Bush, Margaret Dayton, Utah State representative and representatives of other states have challenged the validity of your No Child Left Behind Law over their own state laws. Your No Child Left Behind Law is under funded by the federal government. President Bush, why should state money pay for a federal law that states find ineffective and hurts state budgets?

306. President Bush, would you oppose legislation that would give soldiers affected by stop loss an additional $2,000 per month for each additional month they are forced to serve because of your administration's implementation of stop loss?

307. President Bush, teachers are leaving poor neighborhoods to teach in richer neighborhoods. The teachers do this to increase their wages. This increases the teacher turn over in poor neighborhoods increasing the educational problems of those poor neighborhoods. President Bush, what is your administration doing to lower teacher turnover in poor neighborhoods?

308. President Bush, your administration has borrowed millions and billions of dollars from foreign countries such as China and Saudi Arabia making the United States a debtor nation. Have you considered how the United States will be effected if these countries choose to call in their debts?

309. President Bush, should there be a limit on the number of children women receiving welfare should be permitted?

310. President Bush, you said that you believe that Intelligent Design should be taught in schools along with Evolution. Countries in the Middle East such as Iran, Iraq, and Saudi Arabia teach religion along with science in their schools. President Bush, how is the teaching of religion alongside science different than that practiced in the Middle East? Is there a difference?

311. President Bush, you cut your vacation short to help pass legislation to stop Terry Schiavo's feeding tube from being taken out but you stayed on vacation during the approach of Hurricane Katrina to the Gulf Coast and Katrina's catastrophic hit on the Gulf Coast rather than cutting your vacation short so you could coordinate emergency procedures before Katrina hit. President Bush, why was Terry Schiavo important enough to get you to cut your vacation short but Hurricane Katrina and the thousands of people and property and equipment that it effected was not important enough to get you to cut your vacation short?

312. President Bush, thousands of people died in Louisiana because of Hurricane Katrina. During the time that Katrina hit, most Louisiana National Guardsmen and Guardswomen along with their equipment were in Iraq but if they were in Louisiana, they would have been able to help keep order and many of the people who died because of the Katrina would be alive today. President Bush, hasn't your administration spread the National Guard to thin? How can the National Guard protect the United States from disasters if they and their equipment are in Iraq?

313. President Bush, NAFTA caused hundreds of thousands of American jobs to be sent overseas leaving hundreds of thousands of American families to suffer to make ends meet. Your administration has succeeded in pushing CAFTA through congress. CAFTA is predicted to send hundreds of thousands of more jobs out of the United States adding to the hundreds of thousands of jobs lost by NAFTA and the hundreds of thousands of families devastated because of the ratification of CAFTA. President Bush, have you pushed through CAFTA for the benefit of the families of the United States or have you pushed through CAFTA to increase the profits of Corporations that donate to your administration? Do you care about the potential hundreds of thousands of families that will be adversely affected through the ratification of CAFTA?

314. President Bush, is your administration using the surpluses of Social Security to make the U.S. deficit look smaller? Have you used the Social Security surplus to help fund the Iraq war?

315. President Bush, Vice President Dick Cheney refused to disclose the information he received while in meetings with energy companies. Your administration was sued for the information but the United States Supreme Court sided with your administration; allowing Vice President Dick Cheney to keep information from the talks secret. President Bush, why wouldn't your administration want to make the details of the meeting public so that the American people could see that your administration had nothing to hide? Shouldn't government transparency be the corner stone of a just and honest government?

316. President Bush, your fiscal policies has caused the largest deficit in American history. It has been said that your administration has caused the deficit on purpose because you are following a conservative philosophy called "Starve-The-Beast" that uses deficits to force the government to reduce spending on social programs such as Social Security, Medicare, Medicaid, Section 8 and other American social programs. You have campaigned to change Social Security and your budget has cut funding for Medicaid, Medicare, Section 8 and other social programs. President Bush, is your administration purposely causing American deficits to destroy and eliminate American social programs in accordance to the conservative philosophy "Starving-The-Beast"?

317. President Bush, your administration does not allow prescription drugs to be re-imported from Canada. You said that this policy was put in place to protect the American people from being attacked through the use of those re-imported prescription drugs yet you have done very little to check fruit, vegetables, and other food that is imported into the United States every day. President Bush, do you truly have this policy in place to protect American citizens or has your administration put this policy in place to help increase the profits of the pharmaceutical industry? Hasn't your administration received large donations from pharmaceutical corporations?

318. President Bush, both your election win in 2000 and your re-election win in 2004 are questionable. Your 2000 election win was decided by the United States Supreme Court because of voting irregularities in Florida and your 2004 re-election was questionable because of voting irregularities in both Ohio and Florida.

You preach that you want the governments of the world to become democracies but one of the most important parts of a democracy is fair elections but your administration has done nothing to push through legislation to make sure U.S. elections are fair and transparent. President Bush, how can you seriously preach to countries of the world about democracy when one of the cornerstones of democracy, fair and transparent elections, is not practiced here in the United States?

319. President Bush, you pushed the energy bill through Congress. The bill does nothing to help the American people get relief from high gas prices but it does help corporations increase their profits. President Bush, did you push this bill through Congress to help the American people or to help corporations?

320. President Bush, your administration has considered closing military run schools that educate the children of American soldiers. Why would your administration consider closing schools for the families of soldiers that risked and many times gave their lives to protect America?

321. President Bush, your administration has sought to cut imminent danger pay and family separation pay for active duty soldiers. Your administration has cut funding to VA Hospitals. Your administration has proposed adding a $250 annual charge to veterans with non-service related illnesses that make more than $26,000 per year. Your administration charged soldiers $8 per day while receiving medical treatment for injuries received while in battle in Iraq and Afghanistan. Your administration sought to close military commissaries that helped financially strapped soldiers and their families to afford everyday necessities. President Bush, why is your administration working so hard to hurt the very soldiers that you sent to fight for the interests of America? Knowing this; why should any American join the military?

322. President Bush, many National Guard and Reservists who were mobilized to fight in Iraq and Afghanistan who have waited to receive reimbursement for food and lodging expenses have not been reimbursed interest. Why has your administration not given the National Guard and Reservists that you sent to maybe die for the defense of America the interest money that they deserve?

323. President Bush, your administration has been liberally using stop loss to maintain troop numbers in Iraq. This has been a factor in your administration's

inability to meet its recruitment quotas. President Bush, is your administration using stop loss because it knows that calling for reinstatement of the draft would be political suicide?

324. President Bush, is your administration going to continue to use the stop loss policy that forces active duty soldiers and National Guard personnel to remain in the military even though they fulfilled the terms of their contract?

325. President Bush, your administration's use of stop loss endangers the lives of military personnel past the years included in their contracts. This means that a soldier who signed a contract to stay in the military for two years, for example, but has to stay in the military for three years under stop loss has an excellent chance of dying or getting injured during the additional year that stop loss forces them to serve. President Bush, do you believe that this is fair to the troops that serve our country and if so, why?

326. President Bush, National Guard and Reservists have been hounded by collection agencies because your administration has not reimbursed them for travel, lodging, and food expenses. What will your administration do to protect our National Guard and Reservists from the harassment of collection agencies?

327. President Bush, Border Patrol Uniforms are made in Mexico. Border Patrol personal are U. S. agents. President Bush, shouldn't Government Agent Uniforms be made in the U.S? What would Americans think if the presidential limousine was made in Japan?

328. President Bush, you said "It is true that much of the intelligence turned out to be wrong. As president I am responsible for the decision to go into Iraq." You also said "We cannot and will not leave Iraq until victory is achieved." This revelation means that over two thousand American soldiers have died and many more have been wounded and disabled because of a mistake but you want more to die and be wounded and disabled for the same mistake. President Bush, why should American citizens volunteer to fight in Iraq and risk their lives when they know that the war was born from a mistake?

329. President Bush, you said "It is true that much of the intelligence turned out to be wrong. As president, I am responsible for the decision to go into Iraq." This revelation means that thousands of Iraqis have been killed, wounded, and dis-

abled because of a mistake. Why shouldn't they be furious over the fact that their country was attacked and is now occupied because of a mistake?

330. President Bush, you said "It is true that much of the intelligence turned out to be wrong. As president, I am responsible for the decision to go to Iraq.". But, the Downing Street Minutes show that the intelligence you got was correct but you chose to make the intelligence fit your goal to invade Iraq. President Bush, doesn't the Downing Street Minutes make your statement a lie?

331. President Bush, you were nominated for the Nobel Peace Prize. You have involved the United Stated in war during almost all of your presidency. President Bush, what about you is worthy of Nobel Peace Prize?

332. President Bush, gays are not permitted to serve in the military. They are American citizens. Why shouldn't they have the right to serve just as any other American citizen?

333. President Bush, you signed an executive order allowing the National Security Agency to eavesdrop on American citizens without warrants. President Bush, why isn't this unconstitutional? Why shouldn't American citizens be furious at you and your administration for taking away their civil rights?

334. President Bush, you signed an executive order allowing the National Security Agency to eavesdrop on American citizens without going through the U.S. court system. Upon discovering that The New York Times discovered the executive order and did investigations, your administration asked that the paper not print their discovery. Officials of your administration said that there is sufficient safeguards to protect the rights of the American people. President Bush, after discovering this, why should any American ever believe anything your administration tells them?

335. President Bush, you signed an executive order allowing the National Security Agency to eavesdrop on American citizens without warrants. You asked that The New York Times not to print this discovery because you were afraid that the eavesdropping policy would tip off potential terrorists. President Bush, was the real reason you did not want the article printed because you were afraid that the American people would be so outraged that they would call for an investigation?

336. President Bush, James Tobin, your New England campaign chairman during your 2004 re-election was convicted of jamming Democratic get-out-the-vote phone banks and a ride-to-the-polls line during the Senate race between Democrat Jeanne Shaheen and Republican John Sununu. Republican John Sununu won the race. President Bush, you were elected by the U.S. Supreme Court in 2000 and you won your re-election in 2004 by a close and questionable race by way of the state of Ohio. Why should the American people trust that your presidency is legitimate?

337. President Bush, your administration got the grades of D's and F's by the 9/11 commission who graded your administration's ability to protect the United States from terrorism. Your administration has been given billions of dollars to enact safe guards against terrorism attacks. President Bush, why hasn't your administration spent the money more wisely?

338. President Bush, you were not telling the American people the truth in regard to the vastness of the spying your administration is conducting of Americans. It was found that your administration, via the National Security Agency (NSA), is tapping directly into America's communication system and randomly searching voice and electronic connections of Americans to others. President Bush, knowing this; why should Americans ever believe you when you speak about your administration's efforts to maintain their constitutional rights?

339. President Bush, you and your senior officials have said that the amount of surveillance you conduct via the NSA is limited yet your administration has worked with communication companies to allow access to switches that carry vast amounts of information. This means that your administration must sift through huge amounts of information to find what you are supposedly looking for. President Bush, why shouldn't the American people be concerned that your administration is gathering information from Americans and storing that information for later use?

340. President Bush, your nominee for Supreme Court Justice, Samuel A. Alito, Jr., has said that the Attorney General should be immune from ordering illegal wire taps. He said this while he was a government lawyer for the Reagan administration. He wrote this in regard to a lawsuit against Attorney General John N. Mitchell. President Bush, did you nominate Samuel A. Alilto partial or fully

because of this view and your Executive order allowing the random spying of American citizens?

341. President Bush, your administration launched a propaganda campaign in Iraq that inserted articles in Iraqi newspapers sympathetic to U.S. interests without the knowledge of the Iraqi people. A strong and unencumbered press is one of the cornerstones of a true democracy. President Bush, how can you hope to build a strong democratic Iraq government if you undermine the legitimacy of its press?

342. President Bush, your administration paid to have articles planted in Iraqi newspapers without the knowledge of the Iraqi people who read the articles. You asked The New York Times not to write an article that exposed your administration's efforts to spy on American citizens. These are only two instances that exposed your administration's efforts to influence newspapers. There may be more instances of news manipulation that the American people know nothing about. President Bush, why should the American people and the people of the world trust that you are telling them the truth when your administration works so hard to filter and manipulate the truth?

343. President Bush, your administration, via the FCC and Michael Powell pushed for the consolidation of media companies. There was much public opposition to this decision because the consolidation would stifle the exchange of thought and opinion which is the cornerstone of a free press and a strong democracy. President Bush, knowing this; why would you want to fight for media consolidation?

344. President Bush, the Republicans of the House and Senate have prevented enacting a raise of the Federal minimum wage but seventeen states have overrode the Federal minimum wage and set their own minimum wage and many more states are debating raising their minimum wage. You, like your party, are against the raising the Federal minimum wage. President Bush, what encouraging words can you give families who are fighting to make ends meet under the current Federal minimum wage?

345. President Bush, your party has fought to prevent the raising of the Federal minimum wage. Many say that raising the minimum raise will make it difficult for companies to compete. President Bush, most third world countries and com-

munists and dictator run countries don't have Federal minimum wages and their citizens suffer in deep poverty to the point of starvation. Should Americans suffer in the same way so they can compete with those countries?

346. President Bush, do you believe that the United States needs a mandated Federal minimum wage? Should the Federal minimum wage override the state's minimum wages?

347. President Bush, you showed great outrage when the media made public your administration's program of spying on Americans but you did not show outrage when Valerie Plame's name, a CIA agent, was made public. President Bush, the outing of Valerie Plame could have affected the lives and caused the deaths of many CIA agents who were connected with Valerie Plame; including informants. Why weren't you equally outraged when Valerie Plame's name was made public?

348. President Bush, your administration via the NSA has spied on American citizens by placing cookies on their computers to track their activities on the internet. This action mirrors actitities that would be practiced by dictators to spy on their perceived enemies. President Bush, why have you allowed your administration to practice these activities?

1. Human Rights Watch World Report 2001

www.hrw.org/wr2k/usa/

2. Washingtonpost.com January 23, 2003

Bush Abandons Rule On Limiting ER Use
By Amy Goldstein
www.washingtonpost.com

3. The New York Times

Supreme Court Hears Arguments on Medical Use of
Marijuana November 29, 2004
By Linda Greenhouse
www.nytimes.com

4. The Sacramento Bee

Congress seeks to cut food aid for poor
By Libby Quaid
October 6, 2005
www.sacbee.com

5. Washingtonpost.com

Legalizing Torture Wednesday, June 9, 2004; Page A20
Editorial
www.washingtonpost.com

6. San Francisco Chronicle (Editorial) Associated Press

How a bad bill becomes law
March 13, 2005
www.sfgate.com

Also see bill S256

7. San Francisco Chronicle

Sane-sex marriage ban of 'national importance'
BUSH DIGS IN: He calls for constitutional amendment
By: Marc Sandalow
February 25, 2004
www.sfgate.com

8. The Christian Science Monitor

The private faith of a public man
How religion shapes this presidency
By Francine Kiefer
September 6, 2002
www.csmonitor.com

9. San Francisco Chronicle

SAN FRANCISCO New homeless plan could be
neutralized
Proposed cuts in HUD housing subsidies criticized
By Kevin Fagan
July 8, 2004
www.sfgate.com

San Francisco Chronicle
Governors Oppose Bush's Medicaid Cuts
By Robert Tanner
February 20, 2005
www.sfgate.com

The New York Times
Bush's Class-War Budget
By Paul Krugman
February 11, 2005
www.nytimes.com

The Boston Globe
Fears voiced on Bush Medicare plan
By Globe Wire Services
July 28, 2004
www.boston.com

10. San Francisco Chronicle

How a bad bill becomes law
March 13, 2005
www.sfgate.com

The Christian Science Monitor
The private faith of a public man
How religion shapes this presidency
By Francine Kiefer
September 06, 2005
www.csmonitor.com

11. Washington Post

Bush Allows Some Stem Cell Funding
By Scott Lindlaw and contributing writer
Laura Meckler
August 9, 2001
www.washingtonpost.com

The Christian Science Monitor
The private faith of a public man
How religion shapes this presidency
September 06, 2005

www.csmonitor.com

12. The Sacramento Bee

Congress seeks to cut food aid for the poor
By Libby Quaid
October 6, 2005
www.sacbee.com

The Sacramento Bee
Governors Oppose Bush's Medicaid Cuts
By Robert Tanner
February 20, 2005
www.sacbee.com

SAN FRANCISCO
New homeless plan could be neutralized
Proposed cuts in HUD housing subsidies criticized
By Kevin Fagan
July 8, 2005
www.sfgate.com

The Christian Science Monitor
The private faith of a public man
How religion shapes this presidency
By Francine Kiefer
September 06, 2002
www.csmonitor.com

13. Washington Post

Schiavo Case Puts Face on Rising Medical Costs
By Jonathan Weisman and Ceci Connolly
March 23, 2005
www.washingtonpost.com

14. Washington Post

Schiavo Case Puts Face on Rising Medical Costs
By Jonathan Weisman and Ceci Connolly
March 23, 2005
www.washingtonpost.com

15. The Boston Globe

Bush ally's firm vies for Medicare cards
By Wayne Washington and Susan Milligan
December 12, 2003
www.boston.com

USA TODAY
Affordable remedies ignored as nation's health woes
soar
March 5, 2003
www.USATODAY.com

16. The Boston Globe

Ill weapons workers a GOP issue Bush, senators fight
over payment
By Nancy Zuckerbrod
September 1, 2004
www.boston.com

17. USA TODAY

Two prescriptions for health insurance crisis
By William M. Welch
October 18, 2004
www.USATODAY.com

18. The Washington Times

The age of Autism: New York nixes mercury
By Dan Olmsted
August 31, 2005
www.washingtontimes.com

19. Washington Post

Secret Tapes Not Meant to Harm, Writer Says
By Lois Romano and Mike Allen
February 21, 2005
www.washingtonpost.com

The New York Times
Supreme Court Hears Arguments on Medical Use
of Marijuana
By Linda Greenhouse
November 29, 2004
www.nytimes.com

20. Connecticut Coalition for Universal Health Care

The Case For Single Payer, Universal Health Care
For The United States
By John R. Battista, M.D. and Justine McCabe, Ph.D.
Outline of Talk Given To The Association of State
Green Parties, Moodus, Connecticut on June 4, 1999
www.cthealth.server101.com

21. United Press International

The Age of Autism: New York nixes mercury
By Dan Olmsted
August 31, 2005
www.washingtontimes.com

22. BusinessWeek

A License to Cherry-Pick
By Brian Grow
May 17, 2004
www.businessweek.com

23. Washington Post

EPA Proposal Would Allow Human Tests of Pesticides
By Juliet Eilperin
June 28, 2005
www.washingtonpost.com

24. The New York Times

A Serious Drug Problem
By Paul Krugman
May 6, 2005
www.selectnytimes.com

The New York Times
Industry fights to Put Imprint on Drug Bill
By Sheryl Gay Stolberg and Gardiner Harris
September 5, 2003

25. Connecticut Coalition for Universal Health Care

The Case for Universal Health Care in the United States
By John R. Battista, M.D. and Justine McCabe, Ph.D.
Outline of Talk Given To The Association of State
Green Parties, Moodus, Connecticut of June 4, 1999
www.cthealth.server101.com

26. The New York Times

Bush's Next Target: Malpractice Lawyers

By Steve Lohr
February 27, 2005
www.newyorktimes.com

27. The New York Times

A Serious Drug Problem
By Paul Krugman
May 6, 2005
www.select.nytimes.com

28. The New York Times

Bush's Next Target: Malpractice Lawyers
By Steve Lohr
February 27, 2005
www.nytimes.com

29. The New York Times

A Serious Drug Problem
By Paul Krugman
May 6, 2005
www.nytimes.com

The New York Times
Industry Fights to Put Imprint on Drug Bill
By Sheryl Gay Stolberg and Gardiner Harris
September 5, 2003
www.select.nytimes.com

30.Washington Post

Bush Allows Some Stem Cell Funding
By Scott Lindlaw
August 9, 2001
www.washingtonpost.com

32. The New York Times

White House Seeks Exception in Abuse Ban
By Eric Schmitt
October 25, 2005
www.nytimes.com

The New York Times
Promoting Torture's Promoter
By Bob Herbert
January 7, 2005
www.select.nytimes.com

33. San Francisco Chronicle

How a bad bill becomes law
By The Associated Press
March 13, 2005
www.sfgate.com

34. The New York Times

Lawyers Organizing for Mass Suits Over Vioxx
By Barnaby J. Feder
November 5, 2004
www.nytimes.com

35. The Boston Globe

No deal
As the administration's recovery plan for the Gulf
Coast testifies, George W. Bush is no Franklin
Roosevelt. He's not even a Herbert Hoover.
By David Greenberg
October 2, 2005
www.boston.com

The Washington Times
Halliburton keeps no-bid Iraq pact
Associated Press
October 30, 2003
www.washingtontimes.com

The New York Times
The 2000 COMPAIGN: THE REPUBLICAN
RUNNING MATE; Cheney Is Said to be receiving
$20 Million Retirement Package
BASED ON REPORTING BY LOWELL BERGMAN,
FLOYD NORRIS AND DIANA B. HENRIQUES
AND WRITTEN BY MS. HENRIQUES
www.select.nytimes.com

36. The New York Times

White House Seeks Exception in Abuse Ban
By Eric Schmitt
October 25, 2005
www.nytimes.com

The New York Times
Promoting Torture's Promoter
By Bob Herbert
January 7, 2005
www.select.nytimes.com

37. Idaho Observer

Bush seeks to seal hundreds of vaccine damage cases
December 2002
www.proliberty.com

The New York Times
Lawyers Organizing for Mass Suits Over Vioxx
By Barnaby J. Feder

November 5, 2004
www.nytimes.com

The New York Times
Bush's Next Target: Malpractice Lawyers
By Steve Lohr
February 7, 2005
www.nytimes.com

38. The San Francisco Chronicle

How a bad bill becomes law
The Associated Press
March 13, 2005
www.sfgate.com

39. The New York Times

Democrats Criticize Oil Industry Subsidies
By Reuters
October 29, 2005
www.nytimes.com

40. The New York Times

Some Tie Libby's Case to the Case for the War
By Carl Hulse
October 29, 2005
www.nytimes.com

41. The New York Times

West Presses for Nuclear Agency to Rebuke Iran,
Despite Russian Dissent
By Steven R. Weisman; Nazila Fathi, Contributor
September 23, 2005
www.nytimes.com

42. The New York Times

Connecticut Librarians See Lack of Oversight as
Bigger Danger in Antiterror Law
By Alison Leigh Cowan
September 3, 2005
www.select.nytimes.com

43. The Washington Post

Panel Questions Patriot Act Uses
By Dana Priest
April 28, 2005
www.washingtonpost.com

44. National Review

I Spy
By Robert A. Levy
July 18, 2002
www.nationalreview.com

45. The New York Times

THE STRUGGLE FOR IRAQ: THE HOMETOWNS;
Confronting Their Losses, Ohio Families Are Shaken
By John Kifner; James Dao and Albert Salvato
Contributors
August 5, 2005
www.select.nytimes.com

46. The New York Times

Foreign Affairs; A Tiger by the Tail
By Thomas L. Friedman
June 1, 2001

www.select.nytimes.com

47. The Jewish Journal

Ignoring Opposition to War an Old Story
By Leonard Fein
March 21, 2003
www.jewishjournal.com

48. The New York Times

Sensing the Eyes of Big Brother, and Pushing Back
By Timothy Egan
August 8, 2005
www.nytimes.com

49. The New York Times

Why exactly Do We Want to Hold the Saudis' Hand
By William Grimes
May 21, 2005
www.nytimes.com

Amnesty International
Saudi Arabia
January to December 2002
www.web.amnesty.org

50. The New York Times

Bush Faces Tough Time in South America
By Larry Rohter
November 2, 2005
www.nytimes.com

The New York Times
INTERNATIONAL BUSINESS; A Sinking U.S.

Dollar Dominates the Debate at Davos
By Mark Landler
January 27, 2005
www.nytimes.com

51. The New York Times

The Senate's Chance on Drug Costs
By Editorial Desk
September 29, 2004
www.nytimes.com

52. Executive Order 13303

www.archives.gov

San Francisco Chronicle
As ordered, it's about oil
By Ruth Rosen
August 8, 2005
www.sfgate.com

53. IsraelNationalnews.com

A Turkey Hunt in Israel
By Ruth Matar
January 14, 2004
www.israelnationalnews.com

CBC
THE fifth estate: Conspiracy Theories
The Saudi Connection
Broadcast October 29th, 2003
www.cbc.ca

The Boston Globe
Why bin Laden plot relied on Saudi hijackers

By Charles M. Sennott
March 3, 2002
www.boston.com

55. Business Week online

The Biggest Bomb in Bush's Budget
By Christopher Farrell
February 13, 2004
www.businessweek.com

San Francisco Chronicle
The deafening—and dangerous—silence on taxes
By David Sirota
September 16, 2005
www.sfgate.com

56. San Francisco Chronicle

The deafening—and dangerous—silence on taxes
By David Sirota
September 16, 2005
www.sfgate.com

57. Texas Observer

Nickel and Dimed
By Gabriela Bocagrande
April 9, 2004
www.texasobserver.og

58. Business Week online

The Biggest Bomb in Bush's Budget
By Christopher Farrell
February 13, 2004
www.businessweek.com

The New York Times
A Serious Drug Problem
By Paul Krugman
May 6, 2005
www.nytimes.com

SAN FRANCISCO CHRONICLE
New homeless plan could be neutralized
Proposed cuts in HUD housing subsidies criticized
By Kevin Fagan
July 8, 2005
www.sfgate.com

SAN FRANCISCO CHRONICLE
Governors Oppose Bush's Medicaid Cuts
By Robert Tanner
February 20, 2005
www.sfgate.com

The Sacramento Bee
Congress seeks to cut food aid for the poor
By Libby Quaid
October 6, 2005
www.sacbee.com

59. REUTERS

Charles, Camilla make first Washington visit
By Deborah Zabarenko
November 2, 2005
http://today.reuters.com

60. Fox News.com

Bush Team Acts to Repeal on Unemployment for
Unpaid Family Leave
December 3, 2002

www.foxnews.com

AFL-CIO Work in Progress
December 9, 2002
www.laborstudies.wayne.edu

61. The New York Times

One Man's Opinion
By Stanley Fish
June 30, 2003
www.nytimes.com

62. International Labor Rights Fund

Written Testimony Regarding the Central American
Free Trade Agreement (CAFTA)
Prepared by the International Labor Rights Fund
March 4, 2002
www.laborrights.org

63. Pittsburgh Post-Gazette

Bush economic report praises 'outsourcing' jobs
By Warren Vieth and Edwin Chen
February 10, 2004
www.post-gazette.com

64. Washington Post

Expansion of Medicaid For Evacuees Backed
By Jonathan Weisman
September 29, 2005
www.washingtonpost.com

65. International Labor Rights Fund

Written Testimony Regarding the Central American
Free Trade Agreement (CAFTA)
Prepared by the International Labor Rights Fund
March 4, 2002
www.laborrights.org

66. USA TODAY

Coast Guard plagued by breakdowns
By Mimi Hall
July 5, 2005
www.usatoday.com

67. The Washington Times

Goss says CIA knows where bin Laden is
By United Press International
June 20, 2005
www.washingtontimes.com

The New York Times
Triumph of the Machine
By Paul Krugman
August 1, 2005
www.nytimes.com

68. The Boston Globe

Bush-backers-only policy voters at RNC rallies
By Steve Larese
August 9, 2004
www.boston.com

69. The Washington Post

Postal Service May Be Urged to Privatize
By Mike Allen and Christopher Lee
December 11, 2002
www.washingtonpost.com

70. The National Organization of Women

Legislative Updates
March 2001
www.now.com

71. The Boston Globe

Rebuilding plan paving way for conservative goals
By Rick Klein
September 25, 2005
www.boston.com

72. The New York Times

House Votes to Block Administration's Rules on
Overtime
By Carl Hulse
September 10, 2004
www.nytimes.com

73. The New York Times

The Dark Side of the Moon
By Robert L. Park
September 22, 2005
www.nytimes.com

74. Salon.com

The Pinocchio presidency
By Joe Wilson
March 16, 2004
www.salon.com

75. FOX NEWS.com

An Exclusive Interview With President Bush
Interviewer: Brit Hume
September 23, 2003
www.foxnews.com

77. Center of Budget and Policy Priorities

EXTENDING TAX CUTS WOULD COST 2.1
TRILLION THROUGH 2015
By Joel Friedman, Ruth Carlitz, and David Kamin
Revised February 9, 2005
www.cbpp.org

The New York Times
Bush's Class-War Budget
By Paul Krugman
February 11, 2005
www.nytimes.com

78. The New York Times

MARKET PLACE; Traders Testing Tokyo's
Commitment to the Dollar
By Jonathan Fuerbringer
April 1, 2004
www.nytimes.com

79. The New York Times

Bush: 'We Do Not Torture'
By REUTERS
November 7, 2005
www.nytimes.com

80. The New York Times

Bush: 'We Do Not Torture'
By REUTERS
November 7, 2005
www.nytimes.com

81. The New York Times

Bush: 'We Do Not Torture'
By REUTERS
November 7, 2005
www.nytimes.com

82. UC Berkeley News

Social Security
Richard M. Abrams, Alan J. Auerbach, Jonathan Berk,
Thomas Davidoff, Neil Gilbert, George Lakoff,
Ronald Lee, David I. Levine, Daniel McFadden,
Terrance Odean, Robert Reich, Andrew Scharlach,
www.berkeley.edu

83. FOX NEWS.com

An Exclusive Interview With President Bush
Interviewer: Brit Hume
September 23, 2003
www.foxnews.com

84. FOX NEWS.com

An Exclusive Interview With President Bush
Interviewer: Brit Hume
September 23, 2003
www.foxnews.com

86. The New York Times

No-Bid Contract to Replace Schools After Katrina is
Faulted
By Eric Lipton

www.nytimes.com

87. The New York Times

No-Bid Contract to Replace Schools After Katrina is
Faulted
By Eric Lipton

www.nytimes.com

90. The New York Times

Judge Unseals Medical Files Of Limbaugh
December 24, 2003
www.nytimes.com

CNN.com
Supreme Court allows prosecution of medical
marijuana
By Bill Mears
June 6, 2005
www.cnn.com

91. San Francisco Chronicle

Key to sex education: discipline or knowledge
Advocating abstinence and safe sex talk may both cut
pregnancies
By Vicki Haddock
May 22, 2005
www.sfgate.com

92. AFL-CIO

Overtime pay
www.aflcio.com

93. The New York Times

Purported CIA Operatives Sought in Italy
By THE ASSOCIATED PRESS Victor L. Simpson
contributor

www.nytimes.com

United Press International—The Washington Times
By United Press International
June 20, 2005
www.washingtontimes.com

94. CBS NEWS

Text Of President Bush's Speech
October 7, 2002
www.cbsnews.com

95. The Boston Globe

Bush cuts hit Democratic states, analysis finds
February 12, 2005

www.boston.com

96. The Federal Observer

U.S.'s Dire Financial Future
By Arnaud de Borchgrave
www.federalobserver.com

Center on Budge and Policy Priorities
EXTENDING THE TAX CUTS WOULD COST 2.1
TRILLION THROUGH 2015
By Joel Friedman, Ruth Carlitz, and David Kamin
www.cbpp.org

San Francisco Chronicle
Governors Oppose Bush's Medicaid Cuts
By Robert Tanner
February 20, 2005
www.sfgate.com

San Francisco Chronicle
SAN FRANCISCO
New homeless plan could be neutralized
Proposed cuts in HUD housing subsidies criticized
By Kevin Fagan
July 8, 2005
www.sfgate.com

Business Week online
The Biggest Bomb in Bush's Budget
By Christopher Farrell
February 13, 2004
www.businessweek.com

97. The New York Times

Part-Time Pay for Full-Time Service
By Editorial Desk

March 10, 2005
www.nytimes.com

98. The New York Times

THE WORLD: GLORY DAYS; Missing In Action:
The War Heroes
By Damien Cave
www.nytimes.com

99. Los Angles Times

Prevailing-Wage Curb for Storm Work Ends
By Edwin Chen
October 27, 2005
www.latimes.com

The Boston Globe
No deal
As the administration's recovery plan for the Gulf Coast
Testifies, George W. Bush is no Franklin Roosevelt.
He's not even a Herbert Hoover
By David Greenberg
October 2, 2005
www.boston.com

100. The New York Times

Report Details F.D.A. Rejection of Next-Day Pill
By Gardiner Harris
www.nytimes.com

101. The New York Times

Fading Foliage
By WESTCHESTER WEEKLY DESK
October 23, 2005

www.nytimes.com

The New York Times
NEWS SUMMARY
July 7, 2005

102. Los Angeles Times

Prevailing-Wage Curb for Storm Work Ends
By Edwin Chen
October 27, 2005
www.latimes.com

AFL-CIO
The Bush Administration's FY 2006 Budget
www.aflcio.org

WORKERS WORLD
Homeland union busting
EDITORIAL
www.workers.org

103. St. Petersburg Times

George W.'s evasiveness on flag just won't cut it
By Bill Maxwell
February 6, 2000
www.sptimes.com

104. The New York Times

Scenes From a Meltdown
By David Brooks
October 20, 2005
www.nytimes.com

105. USA TODAY

Bush talks about Social Security solvency
By J. Scott Applewhite
March 11, 2005
www.usatoday.com

106. Rolling Stone

Deadly Immunity
By Robert F. Kennedy, Jr.
June 20, 2005
www.rollingstone.com

107. The New York Times

Abroad at Home; Shallow And Callous
By Anthony Lewis
June 17, 2000
www.nytimes.com

The New York Times
The Nation; When Killing a Juvenile Was Routine
By Stuart Banner
March 6, 2005
www.nytimes.com

108. Fox News

An Exclusive Interview With President Bush
Interviewer Brit Hume
September 23, 2005
www.foxnews.com

The New York Times
In Setback for Bush, Congress Fails to Pass His
Proposals
By Carl Hulse and David Stout

November 18, 2005
www.nytimes.com

109. San Francisco Chronicle

Rumsfeld warns of photos depicting worse abuses
ONE THE HILL: He apologizes, rebuffs calls to step
Down
By Edward Epstein
May 8, 2004
www.sfgate.com

The Seattle Times
Administration stands in way of POWs' Iraq
Compensation
By David G. Savage
February 19, 2005
www.seattletimes.com

110. The New York Times

Report Says Ex-Chief of Public TV Violated Federal
Law
By Stephen Labaton
November 15, 2005
www.nytimes.com

111. ACLU

Interested Persons Memo: Section-by-Section
Analysis of Justice Department draft "Domestic
Security Enhancement Act of 2003," also known as
"Patriot Act II"
February 14, 2003
www.aclu.org

112. The New York Times

The Great Escape
By Craig Unger
June 1, 2004
www.nytimes.com

113. The New York Times

Doctors Objecting to Planned Cut in Medicare Fees
By Robert Pear
November 20, 2005
www.nytimes.com

Washington Post
Bush Abandons Rule on Limiting ER Use
By Amy Goldstein
January 23, 2005
www.nytimes.com

San Francisco Chronicle
Governors Oppose Bush's Medicaid Cuts
By Robert Tanner
February 20, 2005
www.nytimes.com

Bush cuts hit Democratic states, analysis finds
By Susan Milligan
February 12, 2005
www.nytimes.com

Boston Globe
Fears voiced on Bush Medicare plan
By Globe Wire Services
July 28, 2005
www.boston.com

114. The New York Times

Purported CIA Operatives Sought in Italy
By The Associated Press
November 11, 2005
www.nytimes.com

The San Francisco Chronicle
Rumsfeld warns of photos depicting worse abuses
ON THE HILL: He apologizes, rebuffs calls to step
Down
By Edward Epstein
May 8, 2004
www.sfgate.com

The San Francisco Chronicle
Rumsfeld warns of photos depicting worse abuses
ON THE HILL: He apologizes, rebuffs calls to step
Down
By Edward Epstein
May 8, 2004
www.sfgate.com

The New York Times
Bush: 'We Do Not Torture'
By REUTERS
November 7, 2005
www.nytimes.com

The New York Times
Reports Warned C.I.A. on Tactics In Interrogtion
By Douglas Jehl
November 9, 2005
www.nytimes.com

The New York Times
White House Seeks Exemption in Abuse Ban
By Eric Schmitt

October 25, 2005
www.nytimes.com

115. Washington Post

Secret Tapes Not Meant to Harm, Writer Says
By Louis Romano and Mike Allen
February 21, 2005
www.washingtonpost.com

116. CNN.com

Bush pledges to spread democracy
January 20, 2005
www.cnn.com

The San Francisco Chronicle
Rumsfeld warns of photos depicting worse abuses
ON THE HILL: He apologizes, rebuffs calls to step
Down
By Edward Epstein
May 8, 2004
www.sfgate.com

The New York Times
Reports Warned C.I.A. on Tactics In Interrogtion
By Douglas Jehl
November 9, 2005
www.nytimes.com

117. CNN Money

Saudis said to boost oil output
April 19, 2004
www.cnn.com

118. Washington Post

Secret Tapes Not Meant to Harm, Writer Says
By Louis Romano and Mike Allen
February 21, 2005
www.washingtonpost.com

119. USA TODAY

Senate apologizes for not enacting anti-lynching law
By Ana Radelat
June 13, 2005
www.usatoday.com

120. CNN.com

Cheney offended by Amnesty criticism
Rights group accuses U.S. of violations at
Guantanamo Bay
May 31, 2005
www.cnn.com

CNN.com
Rights group leader says U.S. has secret jails
Top GOP senator says Gitmo hearings might be
Appropriate
June 5, 2005
www.cnn.com

121. CNN.com

Cheney offended by Amnesty criticism
Rights group accuses U.S. of violations at
Guantanamo Bay
May 31, 2005
www.cnn.com

CNN.com

Rights group leader says U.S. has secret jails
Top GOP senator says Gitmo hearings might be
Appropriate
June 5, 2005
www.cnn.com

123. Los Angeles Times

Cheney Scolds War Critics as 'Dishonest'
By Edwin Chen
November 17, 2005
www.latimes.com

CNN.com
Bush asks China to expand freedoms
November 20, 2005
www.cnn.com

124. The New York Times

Iran Votes to Block Nuclear Inspections
By THE ASSOCIATED PRESS
November 20, 2005
www.nytimes.com

125. The New York Times

BUYING OF NEWS BY BUSH'S AIDS IS
RULED ILLEGAL
By Robert Pear
October 1, 2005
www.nytimes.com

126. USA TODAY

Senators concerned with anthrax cleaning
November 29, 2001

www.usatoday.com

127. The Washington Post

Cheney Dismisses Critic With Obscenity
By Helen Dewar and Dana Milbank
June 25, 2004
www.washingtonpost.com

128. CNN.com

Bush asked to explain UK war memo
May 12, 2005
www.cnn.com

131. The New York Times

U.S. Is Sued By Connecticut Over Mandates On
School Tests
By Sam Dillon
August 23, 2005
www.nytimes.com

The New York Times
Judge Tosses Out Education Lawsuit
By THE ASSOCIATED PRESS
November 23, 2005
www.nytimes.com

132. Fortune

BIG PHARMA
By Nelson D. Schwartz
November 1, 2005
www.fortune.com

133. The New York Times

Still Searching for a Strategy Four Years After
Sept. 11 Attacks
By Adam Liptak
November 23, 2005
www.nytimes.com

134. Los Angeles Times

GOP's Flu Plan Would Shield Makers
By Richardo Alonso-Zaldivar
November 17, 2005
www.latimes.com

135. The New York Times

Promoting Torture's Promoter
By Bob Herbert
January 7, 2005
www.nytimes.com

The Washington Post
Legalizing Torture
June 9, 2004
www.washingtonpost.com

San Francisco Chronicle
Rumsfeld warns of photos depicting worse abuses
By Edward Epstein
May 8, 2004
www.sfgate.com

Washington Post
CIA Holds Terror Suspects in Secret Prisons
By Dana Priest
November 2, 2005
www.washingtonpost.com

The New York Times
THREATS AND RESPONSES:
INTERROGATIONS; Questioning Terror
Suspects In a Dark and Surreal World
March 9, 2003
www.nytimes.com

The New York Times
Report Warned C.I.A. on Tactics In Interrogation
By Douglas Jehl
November 9, 2005
www.nytimes.com

136. Washington Post

FBI Papers Indicate Intelligence Violations
By Dan Eggen
October 24, 2005
www.washingtonpost.com

ACLU
Interested Persons Memo: Section-by-Section
Analysis of Justice Department draft "Domestic
Security Enhancement Act of 2003," also Known as
The "PATRIOT Act II"
February 14, 2003
www.aclu.org

The New York Times
Connecticut Librarians See Lack of Oversight as
Biggest Danger in Antiterror Law
By Alison Leigh Cowan
September 3, 2005

137. The New York Times

THE 2004 CAMPAIGN: THE CONSTITUENCIES;

Gay Activists In the G.O.P. Withhold Endorsment
By David D. Kirpatrick
September 8, 2004
www.nytimes.com

CNN.com
Bush calls for ban on same-sex marriages
February 25, 2004
www.cnn.com

138. The Boston Globe

Bush cuts hit Democratic states, analysis finds
By Susan Milligan
February 12, 2005
www.boston.com

San Francisco Chronicle
Governors Oppose Bush's Medicaid Cuts
By Robert Tanner
February 20, 2005
www.sfgate.com

139. CNN.com

Bush pledges to spread democracy
January 20, 2005
www.cnn.com

140. Pittsburgh Post-Gazette

Bush economic report praises 'outsourcing' jobs
By Warren Vieth and Edwin Chen, Los Angeles
Times
February 10, 2005
www.post-gazette.com

San Francisco Chronicle
How a bad bill becomes law
March 13, 2005
www.sfgate.com

141. The New York Times

Connecticut Librarians See Lack of Oversight as
Biggest Danger in Antiterror Law
By Alison Leigh Cowan
September 3, 2005
www.nytimes.com

Washington Post
FBI Papers Indicate Intelligence Violations
By Dan Eggen
October 24, 2005
www.washingtonpost.com

ACLU
Interested Persons Memo: Section-by-Section
Analysis of Justice Department draft "Domestic
Security Enhancement Act of 2003," also Known as
The "PATRIOT Act II"
February 14, 2003
www.aclu.org

CNN.com
Bush pledges to spread democracy
January 20, 2005
www.cnn.com

144. CNN.com

Bush pledges to spread democracy
January 20, 2005
www.cnn.com

145. CNN.com

Bush pledges to spread democracy
January 20, 2005
www.cnn.com

San Francisco Chronicle
Rumsfeld warns of photos depicting worse abuses
ONE THE HILL: He apologizes, rebuffs calls to step
Down
By Edward Epstein
May 8, 2005
www.sfgate.com

The New York Times
THREATS AND RESPONSES:
INTERROGATIONS; Questioning Terror
Suspects In a Dark and Surreal World
March 9, 2003
www.nytimes.com

The New York Times
Bush: 'We Do Not Torture'
By REUTERS
November 7, 2005
www.nytimes.com

146. San Francisco Chronicle

SAN FRANCISCO
New homeless plan could be neutralized
Proposed cuts in HUD housing subsidies criticized
By Kevin Fagan
July 8, 2005
www.sfgate.com

The New York Times
A Serious Drug Problem

By Paul Krugman
May 6, 2005
www.nytimes.com

San Francisco Chronicle
Governors Oppose Bush's Medicaid Cuts
By Robert Tanner
February 20, 2005
www.sfgate.com
The Boston Globe
Bush cuts hit Democratic states, analysis finds
By Susan Milligan
www.boston.com

The New York Times
Bush's Class-War Budget
By Paul Krugman
www.nytimes.com

147. UC Berkeley News

Rx for Social Security
By Richard M. Abrams, Alan J. Auerbach,
Jonathan Berk, Thomas Davidoff, Neil Gilbert,
George Lakoff, Ronald Lee, David I. Levine
Daniel McFadden, Terrence Odean, Robert Reich,
Andrew Scharlach
www.berkeley.edu/news

150. Houston Chronicle

FEMA asks media not to take pictures of bodies
By Reuters News Service
September 7, 2005
www.chron.com

151. USA TODAY

Pentagon cost cutting threatens commissaries
By Dennis Camire
April 26, 2004
www.usatoday.com

152. Idaho Observer

Bush seeks to seal hundreds of vaccine damage cases
December 2002
www.idaho-observer.com

San Francisco Chronicle
As ordered, it's about oil
By Ruth Rosen
August 8, 2005
www.sfgate.com

Oakland Press
Bush administration's power grab sets dangerous
precedent
By Paul Krugman
www.theoaklandpress.com

The New York Times
No-Bid Contract to Replace Schools After Katrina is
Faulted
By Eric Lipton
www.nytimes.com

The New York Times
Industry Fights to Put Imprint on Drug Bill
By Sheryl Gay Stolberg and Gardiner Harris
September 5, 2003
www.nytimes.com

The New York Times

Insurers and Drug Makers See Gain in Bush Victory
By Robert Pear
November 5, 2004
www.nytimes.com

Business Journal
Top Air Polluters Tied to Bush Fund-Raising,
Pollution Policy-Making Process
May 6, 2004
www.business-journal.com

153. The Boston Globe

No Deal
As the administration's recovery plan for the Gulf
Coast testifies, George W. Bush is no Franklin
Roosevelt. He's not even a Herbert Hoover
By David Greenbert
October 2, 2005
www.boston.com

The Boston Globe
Firms with Bush ties snag Katrina deals
By Reuters
September 10, 2005
www.boston.com

156. San Francisco Chronicle

One the Public's Right to Know
The day Ashcroft censored Freedom of Information
January 6, 2002
www.sfgate.com

157. The Guardian

Revealed: how oil giant influenced Bush

By John Vidal
June 8, 2005
www.guardian.co.uk

159. The New York Times

Barbara Bush Calls Evacuees Better Off
By THE NEW YORK TIMES
September 7, 2005
www.nytimes.com

161. USA TODAY

Two prescriptions for health insurance crisis
By Wililam M. Welch
October 18, 2004
www.usatoday.com

The Washington Post
Bush Abandons Rule On Limiting ER Use
By Amy Goldstein
January 23, 2005
www.washingtonpost.com

The New York Times
Doctors Objecting to Planned Cut in Medicare Fees
By Robert Pear
www.nytimes.com

San Francisco Chronicle
Governors Oppose Bush's Medicaid Cuts
By Robert Tanner
www.sfgate.com

162. The Galveston County Daily News

Garment worker challenges DeLay

By Marty Schladen
June 6, 2005
www.galvestondailynews.com

163. The Galveston County Daily News

Garment worker challenges DeLay
By Marty Schladen
June 6, 2005
www.galvestondailynews.com

164. The New York Times

Supreme Court hears Arguments on Medical Use of
Marijuana
By Linda Greenhouse
November 29, 2005
www.nytimes.com

165. The Boston Globe

Bush-backers-only policy riles voters at RNC rallies
By Steve Larese
August 9, 2004
www.boston.com

166. The Boston Globe

Bush-backers-only policy riles voters at RNC rallies
By Steve Larese
August 9, 2004
www.boston.com

CNN.com
Bush pledges to spread democracy
January 20, 2005
www.cnn.com

167. The Boston Globe

Bush-backers-only policy riles voters at RNC rallies
By Steve Larese
August 9, 2004
www.boston.com

168. San Francisco Chronicle

How a bad bill becomes law
March 13, 2005
www.sfgate.com

169. The Boston Globe

Bush trims federal workers' raises, cites 'national security'
By Leigh Strope
August 28, 2003
www.boston.com

170. The San Francisco Chronicle

How a bad bill becomes law
March 13, 2005
www.sfgate.com

176. San Francisco Chronicle

New homeless plan could be neutralized
Proposed cuts in HUD housing subsidies criticized
By Kevin Fagan
July 8, 2005
www.sfgate.com

The Boston Globe

No deal
As the administration's recovery plan for the Gulf
Coast testifies, George W. Bush is no Franklin
Roosevelt. He's not even a Herbert Hoover
By David Greenberg
October 2, 2005
www.boston.com

The New York Times
Bush's Class-War Budget
By Paul Krugman
February 11, 2005
www.nytimes.com

The Washington Post
Bush Abandons Rule On Limiting ER Use
By Amy Goldstein
January 23, 2005
www.washingtonpost.com

178. The New York Times

THE REPUBLICANS; The Bush Philosophy:
Resolute, No Matter What
By Richard W. Stevenson
October 26, 2004
www.nytimes.com

179. The Boston Globe

Bush trims federal workers' raises, cites 'national
security'
By Leigh Strope
August 28, 2003
www.boston.com

180. The New York Times

Senators May Try to Block Vote on Nominee for
U.S. Post
By Douglas Jehl
May 26, 2005
www.nytimes.com

181. The New York Times

A Doctrine Left Behind
By Mark Danner
November 21, 2005
www.nytimes.com

182. The New York Times

Powell to Step Down at F.C.C. After Pushing for
Deregulation
By Stephen Labaton
January 22, 2005
www.nytimes.com

183. The New York Times

A Doctrine Left Behind
By Mark Danner
November 21, 2005
www.nytimes.com

The New York Times
Powell to Step Down at F.C.C. After Pushing for
Deregulation
By Stephen Labaton
January 22, 2005
www.nytimes.com

185. The Washington Post

Bush Name Helps Fuel Oil Dealings
By George Lardner Jr. and Lois Romano
July 30, 1999
www.washingtonpost.com

USA TODAY
Bush urges Congress to pass energy bill
By Associated Press
April 16, 2005
www.usatoday.com

186. The New York Times

Abroad at Home; Shallow and Callous
By Anthony Lewis
June 17, 2000
www.nytimes.com

189. The New York Times

THE 2000 CAMPAIGN: THE REPUBLICAN
RUNNING MATE; Cheney Is Said to Be Receiving
$20 Million Retirement Package
August 12, 2000
www.nytimes.com

Los Angeles Times
Cheney Scolds War Critics as 'Dishonest'
By Edwin Chen
November 17, 2005
www.latimes.com

190. The New York Times

THE STRUGGLE FOR IRAQ:
WASHINGTON; Memo Shows Bush Misled

Public, Antiwar Group Says
By Scott Shane
www.nytimes.com

The New York Times
The War President
By Paul Krugman
June 24, 2005
www.nytimes.com

191. The New York Times

THE STRUGGLE FOR IRAQ:
WASHINGTON; Memo Shows Bush Misled
Public, Antiwar Group Says
By Scott Shane
www.nytimes.com

The New York Times
The War President
By Paul Krugman
June 24, 2005
www.nytimes.com

192. Washington Post

The War's Realists
By E. J. Dionne Jr.
July 12, 2005
www.washingtonpost.com

193. NPR

Powell's Cautions on Iraq
By Robert Siegel
April 20, 2005
www.npr.org

196. The Boston Globe

A tarnished image as a war president
By H.D.S. Greenway
April 2, 2004
www.boston.com

198. The New York Times

THE CONFLICT IN IRAQ: THE COMPANY-
—Six Months in Ramadi; Blooded Marines
Sound Off About Want of Armor and Men
By Micahel Moss
April 25, 2005
www.nytimes.com

Support Our Troops
EDITORIAL DESK
May 1, 2005
www.nytimes.com

201. The Raw Story

U.S. changed Iraq policy to begin airstrikes months
before war
By John Byrne
June 30, 2005
www.rawstory.com

202. National Review

War & Peace
By Stephen Moore
September 26, 2003
www.nationalreview.com

203. Times on Line

The secret Downing Street memo
By David Manning
July 23, 2002
www.timesonline.co.uk

205. The New York Times

Veterans and Officials Oppose Hospital Cuts
By Mike Mcintire
September 6, 2003
www.nytimes.com

The Boston Globe
Sanders joins veterans in protesting funding cuts
February 9, 2005
www.boston.com

206. VETERANS FOR PEACE

Dishonorable Discharge
Bush administration slashes veteran's benefits
By Dave Lindorff
November 26, 2003
www.veteransforpeace.org

207. San Francisco Chronicle

Key to sex education: discipline or knowledge
Advocating abstinence and safe sex talk may both
cut pregnancies
By Vicki Haddock
May 22, 2005
www.sfgate.com

VETERANS FOR PEACE
Dishonorable Discharge

Bush administration slashes veteran's benefits
By Dave Lindorff
November 26, 2003
www.veteransforpeace.org

208. VETERANS FOR PEACE

Dishonorable Discharge
Bush administration slashes veteran's benefits
By Dave Lindorff
November 26, 2003
www.veteransforpeace.org

209. VETERANS FOR PEACE

Dishonorable Discharge
Bush administration slashes veteran's benefits
By Dave Lindorff
November 26, 2003
www.veteransforpeace.org

210. VETERANS FOR PEACE

Dishonorable Discharge
Bush administration slashes veteran's benefits
By Dave Lindorff
November 26, 2003
www.veteransforpeace.org

211. VETERANS FOR PEACE

Dishonorable Discharge
Bush administration slashes veteran's benefits
By Dave Lindorff
November 26, 2003
www.veteransforpeace.org

212. The Washington Times

United Press International
Homeless Iraq vets showing up at shelters
By Mark Benjamin
December 7, 2004

213. VETERANS FOR PEACE

Dishonorable Discharge
Bush administration slashes veteran's benefits
By Dave Lindorff
November 26, 2003
www.veteransforpeace.org

USA TODAY
AP
Bush makes case for private accounts
February 28, 2001
www.usatoday.com

214. The New York Times

U.S. Is said to Pay to Plant Articles in Iraq Papers
By Jeff Gerth and Scott Shane
December 1, 2005
www.nytimes.com

215. The New York Times

Photos of Soldiers' Coffins Spark a Debate Over
Access
By Thom Shanker and Bill Carter
April 24, 2005
www.nytimes.com

216. The Boston Globe

Military recruiters target schools strategically
By Charlie Savage
November 29, 2005
www.boston.com

217. Truthout.org

Halliburton Hearing Unearths New Abuse
By Pratap Chatterjee
CorpWatch
June 27, 2005
www.truthout.org

219. San Francisco Chronicle

Halliburton puts off billing Pentagon for troops'
Meals Company awaiting resolution of dispute
Over number served
By Eric Schmitt
February 17, 2004
www.sfgate.com

220. San Francisco Chronicle

Halliburton puts off billing Pentagon for troops'
Meals Company awaiting resolution of dispute
Over number served
By Eric Schmitt
February 17, 2004
www.sfgate.com

221. The New York Times

Purported CIA Operatives Sought in Italy
By THE ASSOCIATED PRESS

November 11, 2005
www.nytimes.com

CNN.com
Cheney offended by Amnesty criticism
Rights groups accuses U.S. of violations at
Guantanamo Bay
www.cnn.com

The New York Times
Report Warned C.I.A. on Tactics In Interrogation
By Douglas Jehl
www.nytimes.com

St. Petersburg Times
Delivering people into the hands of torturers
By Robyn E. Blumner
November 16, 2003
www.sptimes.com

222. The Washington Post

Democrats Criticize Payments to KBR
By Griff Witte
June 28, 2005
www.washingtonpost.com

223. MSNBC

Newsweek World News
A Tortured Debate
By Michael Hirsh, John Barry and Daniel Klaidman
June 21, 2005
www.msnbc.msn.com

225. VETERANS FOR PEACE

Dishonorable Discharge
Bush administration slashes veteran's benefits
By David Lindorff
November 26, 2003
www.veteransforpeach.org

226. CNN.com

Cheney offended by Amnesty criticism
Rights groups accuses U.S. of violations at
Guantanamo Bay
www.cnn.com

The New York Times
Report Warned C.I.A. on Tactics In Interrogation
By Douglas Jehl
www.nytimes.com

St. Petersburg Times
Delivering people into the hands of torturers
By Robyn E. Blumner
November 16, 2003
www.sptimes.com

227. The New York Times

THE CONFLICT IN IRAQ: THE COMPANY-
—Six Months in Ramadi; Blooded Marines
Sound Off About Want of Armor and Men
By Micahel Moss
April 25, 2005
www.nytimes.com

Support Our Troops
EDITORIAL DESK
May 1, 2005

www.nytimes.com

228. Los Angeles Times

More Armored Vehicles in Works
By Mark Mazzetti
December 11, 2005
www.latimes.com

229. San Francisco Chronicle

Rumsfeld: Iraquis Must Defeat Insurgency
By Douglas K. Daniel
June 26, 2005
www.sfgate.com

230. The New York Times

Editorial Observer; A Family Says an
Unexpected Goodbye to a Reluctant Soldier
By Carol E. Lee
September 25, 2004
www.nytimes.com

231. The New York Times

Editorial Observer; A Family Says an
Unexpected Goodbye to a Reluctant Soldier
By Carol E. Lee
September 25, 2004
www.nytimes.com

233. The New York Times

Editorial Observer; A Family Says an
Unexpected Goodbye to a Reluctant Soldier
By Carol E. Lee

September 25, 2004
www.nytimes.com

CNN.com
Definition of silence
By Mark Shields
June 28, 2005
www.cnn.com

234. Washington Post

Democrats Criticize Payments to KBR
By Griff Witte
June 28, 2005
www.washingtpost.com

235. The Boston Globe

Military recruiters target schools strategically
By Carlie Savage
November 29, 2004
www.boston.com

Guardian Unlimited
US army accused of 'return to the draft'
June 3, 2004
www.guardian.co.uk

The New York Times
THE CONFLICT IRAQ: THE TROOPS;
Eight Soldiers Plan to Sue Over Army Tours of
Duty
By Monica Davey
December 6, 2004
www.nytimes.com

The Boston Globe
Iraq report cites poor planning

By Charles Aldinger
September 4, 2003
www.boston.com

The Boston Globe
A tarnished image as a war president
H.D.S. Greenway
April 2, 2004
www.boston.com

237. CNN.com

High pay—and high risks—for contractors in Iraq
April 2, 2004
www.cnn.com

Salary.com
swz.salary.com

239. The New York Times

Live Tracking of Mobile Phones Prompts Court Fights
on Privacy
By Matt Richtel
December 10, 2005
www.nytimes.com

240. The New York Times

Labor Dept. Is Rebuked Over Pact With Wal-Mart
By Steven Greenhouse
November 1, 2005
www.nytimes.com

241. CNN.com

Former FEMA chief Brown off payroll

Ex-director stayed on to help review Katrina response
November 9, 2005
www.cnn.com

243. CNN.com

Brown to start emergency planning consulting
Business
November 24, 2005
www.cnn.com

244. CNN.com

Bush pays tribute to war dead
November 26, 2005
www.cnn.com

245. CNN.com

Bush pays tribute to war dead
November 26, 2005
www.cnn.com

246. CNN.com

Democrats want Cheney-Halliburton probe
June 1, 2004
www.cnn.com

247. BBC News

US concern over war dead photos
April 28, 2004
www.newsvote.bbc.co.uk

249. CNN.com

Democrats want Cheney-Halliburton probe
June 1, 2004
www.cnn.com

252. The New York Times

Promoting Torture's Promoter
By Bob Herbert
January 7, 2005
www.nytimes.com

The Washington Post
Legalizing Torture
June 9, 2004
www.washingtonpost.com

San Francisco Chronicle
Rumsfeld warns of photos depicting worse abuses
By Edward Epstein
May 8, 2004
www.sfgate.com

253. CNN.com

IRAQ: Transition of Power
Audit: U.S. lost track of $9 billion in Iraq funds
January 30, 2005
www.cnn.com

The Boston Globe
Draft report urges UN overhaul after oil-for-food
Scandal
By Nick Wadhams
December 8, 2005

254. The New York Times

Justice Dept. Opens Inquiry Into Leak of Domestic
Spying
By The Associated Press
December 30, 2005
www.nytimes.com

255. The New York Times

Justice Deputy Resisted Parts of Spy Program
By Eric Lichtblau and James Risen
December 31, 2005
www.nytimes.com

256. San Francisco Chronicle

Halliburton puts off billing Pentagon for troops' meals
Company awaiting resolution of dispute over numbers
Served
By Eric Schmitt
February 17, 2005
www.sfgate.com

257. FORTUNE

ANSWER CENTRAL
Will New Bankruptcy Law Stifle Entrepreneurship?
By Louise Witt
www.fortune.com

FORTUNE
ANSWER CENTRAL
Will the New Bankruptcy Law Help or Hurt?
By Louise Witt
www.fortune.com

258. Utah News

Bankruptcy reform legislation likely to pass
President Bush backs bill; opponents call it classism
By Jerry Spangler
April 12, 2005
www.deseretnews.com

259. Baltimore Sun

Eased rules on special ballots battled
By Andrew Zajac
October 23, 2004
www.baltimoresun.com

261. The New York Times

Federal Spending Increases, but More Schools
Will Get Less Money for Low-Income Students
By Michael Janofsky
July 4, 2005
www.nytimes.com

263. The Boston Globe

Secure at home
GLOBE EDITORIAL
May 24, 2005
www.boston.com

264. WORKERS WORLD

Homeland union busting
November 21, 2002
www.workers.org

266. The New York Times

F.A.A. Official Scrapped Tape of 9/11 Controllers'
Statements
By Matthew L. Wald
May 6, 2004
www.nytimes.com

267. The New York Times

After 14 Weeks, Evacuees Settle Into 14th Home
By Jodi Wilgoren
December 13, 2005
www.nytimes.com

268. CNN.com

EDUCATION
Proposed boost for abstinence-only education
February 13, 2004
www.cnn.com

271. Salon.com

Bush's sex fantasy
By Michelle Goldberg
February 24, 2004
www.salon.com

274. Washington Post

Democrats Say 2004 Election System Failed in Ohio
By Dan Balz
June 23, 2005
www.washingtonpost.com

278. BILLINGS GAZETTE

Bush budget would cut law enforcement funds
By Associated Press
February 6, 2005
www.billingsgazette.com

279. USA TODAY

Yet more breaks for fat cats
October 24, 2005
www.usatoday.com

280. USA TODAY

Yet more breaks for fat cats
October 24, 2005
www.usatoday.com

281. INC.

SBA's Budget Cut—Again
By Walter Alarkon
November 21, 2005
www.inc.com

283. The Gainesville Times

Gay club sparks anger at high school
By Alan Sverdlik
February 8, 2005
www.gainesvilletimes

287. Washington Post

Bush Abandons Rule On Limiting ER Use
By Amy Goldstein

January 23, 2003
www.washingtonpost.com

The New York Times
Doctors Objecting to Planned Cut in Medicare Fees
By Robert Pear
November 20, 2005
www.nytimes.com

The Boston Globe
No deal
As the administration's recover plan for the Gulf
Coast testifies, George W. Bush is no Franklin
Roosevelt. He's not ever a Herbert Hover.
October 2, 2005
www.boston.com

Pittsburgh Post Gazette
Bush economic report praises 'outsourcing' jobs
By Warren Vieth and Edwin Chen
February 10, 2005
www.post-gazette.com

288. San Francisco Chronicle

Bush taps Gonzales as the nation's first Hispanic
attorney general
By Terence Hunt
November 10, 2004
www.sfgate.com

289. San Francisco Chronicle

The deafening—and dangerous—silence on taxes
By David sirota
September 16, 2005
www.sfgate.com

291. USA TODAY

Diebold stops top executives from making political
donations
June 8, 2004
www.usatoday.com

292 Washington Post

Bush Suspends Pay Act In Areas Hit by Storm
By Thomas B. Edsall
September 9, 2005
www.washingtonpost.com

297. SEATTLE WEEKLY

The new apparel line
By Rick Anderson
September 16-22
www.seattleweekly.com

298. NATIONAL EDUCATION ASSOCIATION

Cuts Leave More and More Public School
Children Behind
December 2003/January 2004
www.nea.org

The Boston Globe
No Child law irks teachers' unions
By Julia Silverman
November 13, 2005
www.boston.com

299. NATIONAL EDUCATION ASSOCIATION

Cuts Leave More and More Public School

Children Behind
December 2003/January 2004
www.nea.org

The Boston Globe
No Child law irks teachers' unions
By Julia Silverman
November 13, 2005
www.boston.com

300. Washington Post

Vacation Ends and Crisis Management Begins
By Peter Baker
September 1, 2005
www.washingtonpost.com

301. St. Petersburg Times

It's finger-pointing time!
By Robert Friedman
September 18, 2005
www.sptimes.com

302. St. Petersburg Times

It's finger-pointing time!
By Robert Friedman
September 18, 2005
www.sptimes.com

305. The New York Times

Strongly G.O.P. Utah House Challenges Bush's
Signature Education Law
By Sam Dillon
February 16, 2005

www.nytimes.com

306. The New York Times

Feeling the Draft
By Paul Krugman
October 19, 2004
www.nytimes.com

308. The New York Times

When Weakness Is a Strength
By Stephen S. Roach
November 26, 2004
www.nytimes.com

310. San Francisco Chronicle

Bush: Intelligent Design Should be Taught
August 2, 2005
www.sfgate.com

311. The New York Times

Judge Hears Schiavo Arguments, but Does Not Rule
Yet
By Carl Hulse and Maria Newman
March 21, 2005
www.nytimes.com

Washington Post
Vacation Ends, and Crisis Management Begins
By Peter Baker
September 1, 2005
www.washingtonpost.com

312. The Boston Globe

Demands of wars since 9/11 strain National Guard's
efforts
By Bryan Bender
September 2, 2005
www.boston.com

313. New York Daily News

Does U.S. need CAFTA? No
By Bruce Raynor
July 2, 2005
www.nydailynews.com

Pittsburgh Post Gazette
Bush economic report praises 'outsourcing' jobs
By Warren Vieth and Edwin Chen
February 10, 2005
www.post-gazette.com

315. San Francisco Chronicle

Appeals Court sides with Cheney in Lawsuit
By Pete Yost
May 11, 2005
www.sfgate.com

316. The New York Times

Deficits And Deceit
By Paul Krugman
March 4, 2005
www.nytimes.com

317. The Boston Globe

Bush, Kerry on issue of drug importation
The Associated Press
October 7, 2004
www.boston.com

320. VETERANS FOR PEACE

Dishonorable Discharge
Bush administration slashes veteran's benefits
By Dave Lindorf
November 26, 2003
www.veteransforpeace.org

321. VETERANS FOR PEACE

Dishonorable Discharge
Bush administration slashes veteran's benefits
By Dave Lindorf
November 26, 2003
www.veteransforpeace.org

322. U.S. Government Accountability Office (GAO)

January 2005
www.gao.gov

323. Guardian Unlimited

US army accused of 'return to the draft'
June 3, 2004
www.guardian.co.uk/usa

324. Guardian Unlimited

US army accused of 'return to the draft'

June 3, 2004
www.guardian.co.uk/usa

325. Guardian Unlimited

US army accused of 'return to the draft'
June 3, 2004
www.guardian.co.uk/usa

326. U.S. Government Accountability Office (GAO)

January 2005
www.gao.gov

327. The Washington Post

Patrol uniforms 'made in Mexico'
Jerry Seper
June 15, 2004
www.washtimes.com

328. The New York Times

Bush Defends Iraq Strategy Day Before Key Elections
By ASSOCIATED PRESS
October 14, 2005
www.nytimes.com

329. The New York Times

Bush Defends Iraq Strategy Day Before Key Elections
By ASSOCIATED PRESS
October 14, 2005
www.nytimes.com

330. The New York Times

Bush Defends Iraq Strategy Day Before Key Elections
By ASSOCIATED PRESS
October 14, 2005

Times
The secret Downing Street memo
By David Manning
July 23, 2002
www.timesonline.co.uk

331. USA TODAY

Bush, pope, jailed Israeli among 2004 Nobel Peace
Prize nominees
February 13, 2004
www.usatoday.com

332. The Washington Times

United Press International
Bill submitted to allow gays in military
By Pamela Hess
March 3, 2005
www.washtimes.com

333. The New York Times

Bush Lets U.S. Spy on Callers Without Courts
By James Risen and Eric Lichtblau
December 16, 2005
www.nytimes.com

334. The New York Times

Bush Lets U.S. Spy on Callers Without Courts

By James Risen and Eric Lichtblau
December 16, 2005
www.nytimes.com

335. The New York Times

Bush Lets U.S. Spy on Callers Without Courts
By James Risen and Eric Lichtblau
December 16, 2005
www.nytimes.com

336. The Boston Globe

Ex-GOP official convicted of telephone harassment in
jamming
By Anne Saunders
December 15, 2005
www.boston.com

337. The New York Times

9/11 Panel Issues Poor Grades for handling of Terror
By Philip Shenon
December 6, 2005
www.nytimes.com

338. The New York Times

Spy Agency Mined Vast Data Trove, Officials Report
By Eric Lichtblau and James Risen
December 24, 2005
www.nytimes.com

339. The New York Times

Spy Agency Mined Vast Data Trove, Officials Report
By Eric Lichtblau and James Risen

December 24, 2005
www.nytimes.com

340. The New York Times

Alito Memo in '84 Favored Immunity for Top
Officials
By Adam Liptak and David R. Rosenbaum
December 24, 2005
www.nytimes.com

341. The Los Angeles Times

THE CONFLICT IN IRAQ
U.S. Military Covertly Pays to Run Stories in Iraqi
Press
By Mark Mazzetti and Borzou Daragahi
November 30, 2005
www.latimes.com

The New York Times
THE REACH OF WAR: PROPAGANDA;
Military's Information War Is Vast and Often
Secretive
By Jeff Gerth; Carlotta Gall and Ruhulla Khapalwak
December 11, 2005
www.nytimes.com

342. The Los Angeles Times

THE CONFLICT IN IRAQ
U.S. Military Covertly Pays to Run Stories in Iraqi
Press
By Mark Mazzetti and Borzou Daragahi
November 30, 2005
www.latimes.com

The New York Times
THE REACH OF WAR: PROPAGANDA;
Military's Information War Is Vast and Often
Secretive
By Jeff Gerth; Carlotta Gall and Ruhulla Khapalwak
December 11, 2005
www.nytimes.com

The New York Times
Spy Agency Mined Vast Data Trove, Officials Report
By Eric Lichtblau and James Risen
December 24, 2005
www.nytimes.com

343. The Nation

FCC: Public Be Damned
By John Nichols and Robert W. McChesney
May 15, 2003
www.thenation.com

344. The New York Times

States Take Lead in Push to Raise Minimum Wages
By John M. Broder
January 2, 2006
www.nytimes.com

345. The New York Times

States Take Lead in Push to Raise Minimum Wages
By John M. Broder
January 2, 2006
www.nytimes.com

346. The New York Times

States Take Lead in Push to Raise Minimum Wages
By John M. Broder
January 2, 2006
www.nytimes.com

347. The New York Times

Justice Dept. Opens Inquiry Into Leak of Domestic
Spying
By THE ASSOCIATED PRESS
December 30, 2005
www.nytimes.com

The New York Times
Some Tie Libby's Case to the Case for the War
By Carl Hulse
October 29, 2005
www.nytimes.com

348. The New York Times

Spy Agency Removes Illegal Tracking Files
By THE ASSOCIATED PRESS
December 29, 2005
www.nytimes.com

978-0-595-39040-3
0-595-39040-4